The Bible and the End of the World:
Should We Be Afraid?

The Bible
and the End of the World:
Should We Be Afraid?

Margaret Nutting Ralph

Paulist Press
New York/Mahwah, N.J.

Book design by Joseph E. Petta

Cover design by Cindy Dunne

Library of Congress Cataloging-in-Publication Data

Ralph, Margaret Nutting.
    The Bible and the end of the world : should we be afraid? / Margaret Nutting Ralph.
      p.   cm.
    ISBN 0-8091-3756-9 (alk. paper)
    1. Bible—Prophecies—End of the world. 2. End of the world—Biblical teaching. 3. Bible—Criticism, interpretation, etc. I. Title.
BS649.E63R35   1997
220.1′5—DC21   97-37543
                                                                                    CIP

Published by Paulist Press
997 Macarthur Boulevard
Mahwah, New Jersey 07430

Printed and bound in the
United States of America

Contents

Acknowledgments

I first thought of writing this book after I was asked to give a talk on the theme for Catechist Sunday, 1995: "Imagine God's Mercy." I would like to thank the Education Department of the USCC for suggesting that we do just that. In addition to thanking my editor at Paulist Press, Rev. Lawrence Boadt, I would like to thank my editor at home, Tony Ralph, who read every word of this manuscript and offered many valuable suggestions.

Finally, I would like to thank my parents, husband, children, family, friends, teachers: all who have loved me. I know that it is because I have been faithfully loved that I am able to believe that God loves.

"To each of you I say, 'I thank my God whenever I think of you; and every time I pray for all of you I pray with joy, remembering how you have helped to spread the good news' " (Phil 1:3–4).

They asked him, "Teacher, when will this be, and what will be the sign that this is about to take place?" And he said, "Beware that you are not led astray, for many will come in my name and say, 'I am he!' and 'The time is near!' Do not go after them." (Lk 21:7–8)

"Modern man listens more willingly to witnesses than to teachers, and if he does listen to teachers, it is because they are witnesses."
—Paul VI, *On Evangelization in the Modern World*

Preface

Did you read the quotation which prefaced this book? It was, "They asked him, 'Teacher, when will this be, and what will be the sign that this is about to take place?' And he said, 'Beware that you are not led astray, for many will come in my name and say, "I am he!" and "The time is near!" Do not go after them'" (Lk 21:7–8). You can tell from that passage that this book is written to disagree with those who would instill fear in others by predicting that the "end of the world" is near.

If I agreed with such "doomsayers" I might have begun this book by quoting: "Amen, I say to you, this generation will not pass away until all these things have taken place" (Mt 24:34).

In other words, no matter which side of the argument I am on, I can quote Scripture to support my point of view.

There is nothing wrong with quoting Scripture to support one's point of view. We all do it. We have been doing it for hundreds, even thousands of years. We do this because Scripture has authority in our minds and hearts. We believe that it is revelation and that its authors were inspired. We turn to it for guidance and for knowledge.

However, the fact that we can support opposite points of view by quoting Scripture illustrates the fact that what Scripture actually teaches and what we use the words of Scripture to support may be two very different ideas. When we use Scripture to support our own thinking, we may be failing to teach what Scripture teaches, and instead be using the words and images of Scripture to say something different than what the inspired author used the words and images to say.

In our time, as in times past, many people are using Scripture to instill fear in others. These people claim to know what even Jesus didn't know—the timing of the second coming (see Mt 24:36). This book is written not only to calm the fears which such tactics might stir up, but also to equip you to understand and explain why those who use Scripture to claim such knowledge and to teach a message of fear are simply wrong.

"Wrong?" Isn't that strong language? After all, the Bible is a living word. It contains hidden meaning which may be understood only in hindsight. How can we say that those who use the Bible to instill fear about the "signs of the times," about "the end of the world," are wrong?

It is true that no person, no group of scholars, no faith filled community, no interpretive voice can exhaust the wisdom in Scripture. The most insightful interpretation which I or any other person might give to a passage cannot exhaust the meaning of that passage.

However, it is also true that some interpretations given to a passage are simply wrong. It is possible to be right when you say, "The passage you are quoting is not saying what you claim it is saying."

In this book we will look at a number of passages which have been misinterpreted regularly and which have resulted in people imagining God as an all-powerful, irate parent who is easily insulted and who would withdraw love and punish eternally. We will look at passages which have given some the mistaken idea that certain people have received a spiritual gift which has enabled them to prognosticate inevitable future events. We will look at passages that have caused many to imagine God as unloving and unforgiving. In each case we will explain the reason for the misinterpretation as well as offer a valid interpretation. Even though the revelation which Scripture teaches us cannot be exhausted, nevertheless it can be known. God is love. God loves us. God saves. We will demonstrate that interpretations which deny these central truths are, in fact, misinterpretations. Once passages which appear to deny the revelation of God's love are reinterpreted we will turn our attention to passages which assure us that God is love, that God is about saving, not condemning. The core revelation in both the Old and New Testaments, the old and new covenants ("testament" means "covenant"), is that God loves us. We will look at what Jesus, the revelation of God's love, is pictured as saying about the kingdom of God and the end of the world.

Finally, as people who live before the "second coming," we will hear what Scripture has to tell us about the "in between times." How should we conduct ourselves? Should we live in fear? Were those who lived at the time of the historical Jesus, or those who will live at the time of the second coming, more fortunate than we? Where is the risen Christ now?

In order to answer these questions we will turn to the appearance stories and to John's Gospel. The Gospels tell us that after Jesus' resurrection, when Jesus appeared to his followers, even those who knew him best consistently failed to recognize him. Is the same true of us? Are we aware of Christ in our midst, the Christ who can teach, heal, forgive sin, and unite us in love to each other and to God? Or are we living in fear, listening to those who claim to see the future, becoming more and more disquieted, less and less filled with peace and with joy?

Scripture teaches us that Christ is in our midst. As we learn more about the revelation which Scripture contains, we will grow in our ability to recognize the risen Christ who says, "Be not afraid. I am with you always."

Chapter 1

How to Understand
What You Read
in the Bible

In the Acts of the Apostles we read that the Holy Spirit directed Philip to approach an Ethiopian eunuch who was reading the prophet Isaiah. Philip asked the eunuch, "Do you understand what you are reading?" The eunuch replied, "How can I unless someone guides me?" (Acts 8:30–31). Many of us can identify with the eunuch. We long to grow in our knowledge and love of God. We turn to Scripture because we believe that it contains the good news which our hearts long to hear, but we become frustrated. Often what we read does not sound like good news at all. We find ourselves asking, "Could I be understanding this correctly?" To make things worse, when we turn to others for help we often encounter people who claim to understand Scripture but who use it to promote their own ideas, their own agendas, even to spread their own fears.

Those of us who are alive in the closing years of this millennium have been greatly blessed in that we have been given many people to guide us in understanding Scripture. Since 1943, with the publication of *Divino Afflante Spiritu,* we have had clear direction on how one should approach Scripture in order to understand the revelation which the books in the Bible offer us. In the Vatican II document *Dei Verbum,* in the recent *Catechism of the Catholic Church,* and in the work of many gifted Scripture scholars, we have been given the guidance we need to discern what is a valid interpretation of a scriptural passage and what is not.

In this first chapter we will review the foundational information which is necessary for us to be able to understand Scripture. The material in this chapter is background knowledge for those who are unfamiliar with the difference between what is called a "contextualist" approach to Scripture as compared to a "fundamentalist" approach to Scripture. The method of Scripture interpretation described in this chapter will be applied in every other chapter.

Contextualists and Fundamentalists

Before I define the words "contextualist" and "fundamentalist," or explain how a contextualist differs from a fundamentalist, I would like first to say a few words about what is *not* the difference between them. The difference is not that one believes that the Bible is revelation and the other does not. The difference is not that one believes the biblical authors are inspired and the other does not. The difference is not that one believes the Bible is a living word that corrects, guides, and comforts individuals who come to it with hearts open to the Holy Spirit, and the other does not. Both contextualists and fundamentalists believe that the Bible is the inspired word of God. The difference is in how one goes about listening to that inspired word, how one goes about hearing that word so that it is God's word and not our own misunderstandings which we take away with us.

A contextualist is a person who knows that in order to understand the revelation which any passage of Scripture contains one must read the passage in the context in which it appears in the Bible. A fundamentalist, in the way I am using the word, is a person who does not consider context in his or her search for meaning.

There are three basic contexts which one must consider. These will be named and explained shortly. But first some further background information is necessary. We need to address such questions as: "What is a Bible?" "How did the Bible which we now have come into existence?" "What do we mean when we claim that the Bible is revelation?" "What do we mean when we claim that the Bible is inspired?" "What do we mean when we say that the Bible contains the 'truth?'" When the answers to these questions are understood it will be much easier to appreciate why it is necessary to consider the context of biblical passages in order to hear the revelation which they contain.

What Is a Bible?

The word "Bible" means, "a collection of books." In other words, the Bible is not a single book with a number of chapters, but a library of books. As in any library, the books are by a variety of authors who lived at a variety of times in history and who lived in a variety of social settings. Also, as in any library, the books represent a variety of literary forms. We will talk more about the ramifications of these facts when we discuss the contexts which one must consider in order to correctly understand the revelation which the Bible contains.

How Did the Bible Come into Existence?

Moses had no Bible to read. The great prophets could not have read the early books of the Bible in the form in which we now have them. Jesus' first century disciples could not have read the New Testament in the form in which we now have it. Our Bible is the end product of a five step process which took two thousand years. It is the result of the members of the believing community of each generation reflecting on the experience of God acting in their midst and passing on their reflections to the next generation.

Events

The first step in this five step process is events. God revealed God's self not through dictation to a chosen individual but through mighty acts in the midst of the community. These acts occurred over a period of two thousand years, starting with Abraham, who lived around 1850 B.C., and ending with the close of the first century after Jesus' resurrection. Throughout history God acted in the lives of God's people, calling Abraham and the patriarchs to the promised land, calling Moses to lead his people out of slavery in Egypt, uniting the twelve tribes under King David, calling the people to fidelity through the great prophets as first the Northern Kingdom and then the Southern Kingdom were defeated by political enemies, comforting the people during their exile in Babylon, calling them back to the Holy Land,

EVENTS BEHIND ORAL AND
WRITTEN TRADITIONS

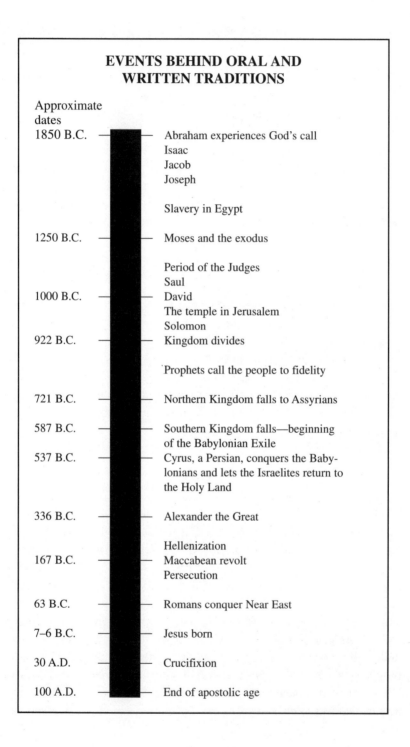

Approximate
dates

1850 B.C. ——— Abraham experiences God's call
Isaac
Jacob
Joseph

Slavery in Egypt

1250 B.C. ——— Moses and the exodus

Period of the Judges
Saul
1000 B.C. ——— David
The temple in Jerusalem
Solomon
922 B.C. ——— Kingdom divides

Prophets call the people to fidelity

721 B.C. ——— Northern Kingdom falls to Assyrians

587 B.C. ——— Southern Kingdom falls—beginning
of the Babylonian Exile
537 B.C. ——— Cyrus, a Persian, conquers the Babylonians and lets the Israelites return to
the Holy Land

336 B.C. ——— Alexander the Great

Hellenization
167 B.C. ——— Maccabean revolt
Persecution

63 B.C. ——— Romans conquer Near East

7–6 B.C. ——— Jesus born

30 A.D. ——— Crucifixion

100 A.D. ——— End of apostolic age

challenging them through these events to rethink their traditions, to rethink their understanding of covenant love, to come to new depths of understanding about God's love and God's purposes. Through the great sweep of history God prepared God's people to receive, to know, and to understand the unbelievable depth of God's love which was fully revealed in Jesus Christ. After Jesus' resurrection revelatory events continued. Through the inspiration of the Holy Spirit the early Church continued to experience God's self-revelation through events, continued to reflect on their experiences, and continued to pass on their insights to their contemporaries and to their descendants.

Oral Tradition

The second step in the process that resulted in our present Bible is oral tradition. As people experienced God's power and presence in the events of their lives they talked about their experiences. Right at this point in the process a variety of "literary forms," a variety of ways of talking about the insights gained from experience, developed. The story tellers were not acting as historians, motivated by a desire to give future generations the answer to the question, "Tell me exactly what happened." Rather they were Spirit-filled members of the community who wanted to share with others what they were able to understand about the significance of events. While they gained their insights through reflecting on events, those insights could be taught through any number of literary forms, including legends, poems, letters, battle cries, myths, allegories, dirges, oracles, debates, songs, laws, parables, fiction, creeds—any literary form at all. No matter what the form, the story teller's motivation was to pass on the truth, revealed through events and known through the inspiration of the Holy Spirit, so that his contemporaries could see their own lives in the context of covenant love.

Since so many modern day readers of the Bible bring to their reading the false presumption that the Bible contains only one kind of writing, history, it seems wise to address the question, "What is the relationship between the revelatory event and the account of that event as it appears in Scripture?" The answer to the question differs depending on the literary form used. A legend is closer to historical writing than many forms although it does not claim to provide exact quotations, exact historical chronology, or exact social settings. Nevertheless, at the core of the account is an event that proved revelatory. A debate is the composition of an author, not a claim to have overheard the reported discussion. Nevertheless a debate is related to events in that the insights which the author places on the lips of the debaters are insights which the author learned by reflecting on events. A fiction story has the least correlation to an actual event, but even in the case of fiction the insight which the author is teaching his contemporaries is an insight learned from events, learned from God's mighty actions in the midst of God's people. So no matter what the literary form used, the insights taught through the form are related to events in that they were gained through reflecting on events.

GROWTH PROCESS

Events	God reveals God's self through events.
Oral Tradition	People talk about these events.
Written Tradition	Parts of the oral tradition are gradually written down (i.e., songs, riddles, stories about individual people, etc.).
Edited Tradition	At various times in history people collect and edit oral and written traditions.
Canonical	Some of these edited traditions are recognized by the worshiping community as inspired and are accepted as vehicles of revelation because they faithfully reflect the experience and beliefs of the community.

Written Tradition

The third step in the process that resulted in the Bible as we now have it is written tradition. At various times in history parts of the oral tradition were written down. Perhaps a victory song would be written, or laws, or creeds, or genealogies, or legends about ancestors that taught succeeding generations the truths about God's love. Various units of the oral tradition were written to serve the needs of the generation contemporary with the writer. Such writing would be handed down, copied and revised to fit the needs of succeeding generations.

Editing

At various times in history people would collect the inherited oral and written traditions of the people and edit them into a unified whole. The editing did not occur only once. It occurred and recurred as the centuries passed. At the time of King David such an editing took place. A second editing took place soon after from the point of view of the Northern Kingdom. Editors went over the whole tradition again at the time of King Josiah. Still another editing occurred after the Babylonian Exile. In regard to New Testament materials, Mark, Matthew and Luke are all editors who have arranged the inherited oral and written traditions about Jesus' public ministry, death and resurrection in a certain order for certain audiences. The editors arranged and edited the inherited materials in the light of subsequent events and in the light of the needs of their contemporaries. The motive was always to help their contemporaries understand and respond to God's love.

Canonical

Not all of the literature which developed through these four steps is in the Bible. The books that are in the Bible are called "canonical," those that are not are called "apocryphal." The word "canon" originally referred to a measuring stick or a ruler. The books of the Bible are canonical because they are the "rule" of faith. These are the books which the believing community over the centuries claimed faithfully passed on their beliefs and consistently nourished their faith from generation to generation. The canon was not chosen on a single occasion or even by a single generation. The canon developed slowly over the centuries. It was defined at particular times in history: after the Babylonian Exile, after a first century Jewish council called the Council of Jamnia, during the second, third and fourth centuries as the early Church Fathers compared notes on what was becoming the norm in the various Christian communities, at the Council of Trent, in the 16th century, after a question arose about whether some books generally accepted should be excluded. However, all the definitions or "closings" of the canon were affirmations of what had become normative through the action of the Holy Spirit in the lives of generations of believing communities. It was the believing communities who decided that these books contained revelation.

What Is "Revelation"?

What do we mean when we claim that the Bible is revelation? A disagreement on this subject has caused many an argument between contextualists and fundamentalists. When we claim that the Bible is revelation we are not claiming that the meaning which we impose on words taken out of context is the meaning which God or the biblical authors intended us to understand. Nor are we claiming that the inspired biblical authors had supernatural knowledge on every subject, knowledge about astronomy, biology, history, or even about future events which others of their generation knew nothing. When we claim that the Bible is revelation we mean that it teaches us what we need to know to be in right relationship with God, to know that God loves us, and to know what God would have us do to build up God's kingdom rather than to tear it down.

I know that I actually do believe that the Bible is revelation because my belief enables me to make an astounding statement. Even though I am a person of very limited knowledge because I have lived at only one time in history, I have lived in only one country, I can see things only from the point of view of a white, middle-aged woman, nevertheless I believe that I know what God would have me do. Think of it! I believe that I know something about the nature of God and about the will of God. These are absolutely astounding statements! How could I possibly claim to know what is so totally beyond my comprehension? My boldness to make such statements is a ramification of the fact that I believe that the Bible is revelation. I can know such things because for centuries God has chosen to reveal God's self to God's people through events, to inspire people to understand the significance of those events, and to pass on their insights to others. I, along with the whole Church, am the recipient of this revelation.

What Is Inspiration?

When we say that the Bible is the fruit of inspiration, or that the biblical authors are inspired, we are claiming that God is the author behind the human authors. We are claiming that the insights which the biblical authors received are the result of the action of the Holy Spirit in their minds and hearts. However, now that we know the five steps which preceded the Bible as we now have it, we may have to broaden our idea of inspiration. Inspiration did not start with the writer. Rather, inspiration started with those who experienced the original events and were able to discern God's presence, power, and purpose in those events. Inspiration continued with each generation as the oral tradition passed on accounts of events and lessons learned from those events to each succeeding generation. Inspiration continued with the editors who reviewed the inherited oral and written traditions in the light of subsequent events, and who went over the whole tradition up to their own time in order to tell the stories as a connected whole. Inspiration continued as the Holy Spirit filled the believing communities who received the stories so that they could understand them, treasure them, be fed by them, apply them to their own settings, and pass them on to the next generation. Inspiration continues even now as those of you who long to better understand God's word read books such as this to help you in your search. That longing is a gift of the Holy Spirit. Now the Holy Spirit is inspiring our generation to play our part in listening, applying, and passing on the inspired word of God to our own and to the next generation.

Is the Bible True?

Both contextualists and fundamentalists would, of course, claim that the Bible is true. However, we may disagree on what we mean by that claim. A contextualist would not use the word "truth" as a synonym for "historically accurate" or "scientifically accurate." A contextualist would claim that the Bible is true because what the Bible teaches is true. Truth can be taught through historical and scientific writing, but it can also be taught through any other kind of writing. Every literary form can be the vehicle for truth, for revelation. So a contextualist would see no contradiction in claiming that, while a particular story in the Bible does not purport to be historically accurate, it nevertheless is true because what the story teller is teaching through the story is true.

Another word, in addition to "truth," which sometimes causes misunderstandings between contextualists and fundamentalists is the word "literal." Are the stories in the Bible literally true? Fundamentalists sometimes accuse contextualists of not taking the Bible "literally." As a contextualist I claim that I do take the Bible literally. However, what I take literally is what the biblical author is teaching, not the literal meaning of the words taken out of context.

An example may help to clarify this point. Say that I told you that there had been a drought, that I had prayed for rain, and that it had rained cats and dogs. If you were to understand me literally what would you have understood me to say? If you took the words literally, rather than understanding the intent of the speaker, you would think that carcasses had fallen from the sky. If you took the intent literally you would think that it had rained hard, rather than just sprinkled. When it comes to the Bible, the contextualist takes the teaching literally, takes the intent of the author literally, as distinct from the meaning of the words separated from their context. The contextualist takes literally such difficult teachings as "Love your enemy." However, the contextualist does not believe that one can presume to know the meaning of words unless one considers their context.

Three Contexts To Be Considered

There are three contexts which must be considered in order to determine the revelation which any passage of Scripture is teaching. These contexts are the literary form, the beliefs of the time, and the process of revelation. We will now explain each of these contexts in detail.

The Literary Form

As was stated earlier, the Bible is a library of books written in a variety of literary forms. In order to understand the revelation which any book in the Bible contains one must consider the literary form, because the intent of the author is determined by the form. To misunderstand the form is to misunderstand the intent and, when one is speaking of the Bible, to misunderstand the revelation.

This necessity of understanding form in order to understand intent was illustrated several years ago in my hometown of Lexington,

---

A CONTEXTUALIST

Reads Scripture passages in context.

- What is the literary form?
- What is the social context within which the author is addressing the audience?
- How does this writing fit into the process of revelation which we find in the Bible?

Kentucky, due to a misunderstanding of the literary form of a letter to the editor. The social context of the letter was that the Supreme Court had ruled that homosexual activity between two consenting adults in the privacy of their home would be illegal. A person who disagreed with this ruling chose the literary form of a satiric letter to the editor to express his opinion. The letter suggested that left-handedness should be declared illegal. The writer went on to say that left-handed people are very annoying. One need only sit next to one at a dinner party to understand why. Obviously God did not intend that anyone be left-handed or all those little desks in grade school would not have had the writing side on the right side.

As it turned out, many left-handed people in the Lexington area did not have an ear for satire. Many were insulted by the letter, so insulted that they, too, wrote letters to the editor expressing their outrage that anyone would suggest that left-handedness be declared illegal. The newspaper did not explain the misunderstanding. Instead it regularly printed letter after letter vociferously upholding the rights of left-handed people. The issue was laid to rest after a front page story reported that a doctor in California had been arrested for receiving human brains in the mail for the purpose of medical research. This story prompted another letter to the editor which suggested that since brains were being mailed across the country, somewhere there must be some empty heads. The writer thought that some of the empty heads were undoubtedly located in the Lexington area.

The whole discussion about the legality of being left-handed was ridiculous because it was irrelevant. The legality of being left-handed was not a social issue, but the legality of homosexual activity between consenting adults was. It was that issue which needed to be debated, but it was ignored. This is exactly what happens with the Bible. When people misunderstand the literary form of a book of the Bible they completely misunderstand what the book is about. As a result they start to discuss at length things that are totally irrelevant to the intent of the author, thus not only wasting their time but failing to hear the revelation which that book of the Bible teaches. Since most people read the Bible in order to hear the revelation, this is a huge loss indeed.

One way to tell if a person has misunderstood the literary form of a book in the Bible, and so has begun to discuss "the legality of left-handedness," is to ask yourself whether the subject being discussed is pertinent to revelation. When you hear someone discuss whether God could make a snake talk or whether a person could survive in the belly of a fish for three days you are hearing a discussion about the legality of being left-handed. Such people have misunderstood the literary form and are discussing irrelevancies, thus sparing themselves the painful topics with which the biblical authors intended to confront us, topics such as whether or not sin always causes suffering and whether or not God loves our political enemies. These are the topics which need to be discussed. When we misunderstand the literary form we avoid them.

Let one more example serve to demonstrate the importance of understanding literary form. Our culture is familiar with the form

LITERARY FORM

Answers the question: —"What kind of writing is this?"

When we say a work is one   —External Characteristics
particular form we are   Poetry?
describing such things as   Prose?
                                         Number of Lines?
                                         Rhyme scheme?
                                     —Internal Characteristics
                                         Attitude?
                                         Tone?
                                         Purpose?

Some possible forms are   —Riddle   Epic
                                        Poem   Mock Epic
                                        Fiction   Sonnet
                                        Myth   Elegy
                                        Legend   Epigram
                                        Parable   Blessing
                                        Biography   Curse
                                        Autobiography Fable
                                        Parody   Fairy Tale
                                        Editorial   Romance
                                        History   Satire
                                        Letter   Proverb
                                        Revelation   Midrash
                                        Allegory   Oracle
                                        Debate   Novel

If we misunderstand the form we misunderstand the meaning!

"debate." If you were to write a debate you would have to write two sides of an argument. You would have to write the side with which you personally disagree with as much persuasiveness as you write the side with which you agree. Otherwise you have not written a good debate. The author of the book of Job chose the literary form of debate to challenge a belief of his time, that all suffering is due to sin. Since he is writing a debate, the author has to place the argument with which he disagrees on the lips of one of his characters. Now, say that you did not know that Job is a debate. Instead of reading the book from the beginning you simply open it up in the middle and read part of one of Eliphaz's speeches. Eliphaz, contrary to the inspired author, believes that all suffering is due to sin. So if you were to take Eliphaz's speech out of context and assume that the words you are reading express the intent of the author, you would be putting the authority of Scripture behind an idea which the book was written to teach against. To misunderstand the form is to misunderstand the intent and the revelation.

A common reaction which many people have after learning that they must consider literary form in order to understand any book in the Bible is to feel intimidated. Many ask, "Why is this so hard? Wasn't the Bible meant to be understood by everyone? How am I supposed to be able to tell one literary form from another?" The stories in the Bible are meant to be understood by the general population. They are popular literature. Most people have no difficulty distinguishing among literary forms once they know that they should. Indeed, they do it every day when they read a newspaper. We all know the difference between a front page story, an editorial, an advice column, a cartoon, and a feature article. We also know how to change our expectations, how to change what we expect from an author, depending on the literary form which the author has chosen.

The problem many have when reading the Bible is that they have not given themselves permission to distinguish among literary forms. So when an author gives a reader hints about the literary form, such as picturing a snake talking, the reader says, "Well, God can do anything." I am perfectly willing to agree that God can do anything. However, if we apply that concept to a story in which the author is not claiming that God can do anything, but instead is informing us about the literary form, we are simply failing to understand the revelation which the author intended to teach us. Form—intent—revelation: the three are connected. We will miss the revelation if we ignore the form and the intent.

The Beliefs of the Time

A second context which must be considered is the beliefs of the time of the author. Every inspired biblical author lived at a particular time in history, in a particular social context, with others of the author's generation. The fact that the author was inspired means that the author had spiritual insight, understood truths about God's nature, the relationship of human beings to God and each other, and what God would have us do. It does not mean that the author had knowledge beyond the knowledge of the author's generation in scientific areas such as geology, biology or psychology. For instance, an inspired biblical author who lived at a time when everyone thought the world was flat also thought that the world was flat. The fact that the author was inspired did not give the author God's knowledge on every subject under the sun. The ramification of this fact is that when we read the work of an inspired author we must learn to separate the author's teaching from the author's presumptions. The teaching is the revelation; the presumptions are not.

Let me give you an example. Say that an inspired author was overwhelmed with an experience of God's love, power, and beauty as he stood beside the sea. He had a keen understanding of the fact that the whole created order was a reflection of God's love, an extravagant gift of love to God's people. He wanted to pass on this insight to others. Say that such a person lived in 450 B.C. He might begin his story by saying, "God made dust out of nothing, rolled it out with a rolling pin, placed it on four posts and named it earth." If the same inspired author with the same experience, the same insight, and the same desire to pass on the truth which he had perceived lived in our century he might begin his story by saying, "God made dust out of nothing, rolled it into a ball, placed it in the firmament and named it earth." From the point of view of revelation, these two stories are identical and are equally true. Neither story purports to be scientific. Each is teaching exactly the same thing about the relationship between God and the created order. The author's mistaken presumption about the shape of the earth is irrelevant to the truth which he is teaching. What the author intends to teach is true.

This is the case with biblical authors. The point which they are teaching is true. However, in the course of elaborating on that point or applying that point to the lives of the author's contemporaries, the author may include some presumptions of the time which later generations realize are in error.

Throughout history various individuals who were right have been persecuted by well-meaning but mistaken Bible lovers who were unable to make the distinction between an inspired author's teaching and his presumptions. The excommunication of Galileo, who said that the sun, not the earth, is the center of the movement of the planets, is a case in point. The Scopes trial, in which a high school science teacher was accused of teaching something contrary to revelation when he taught Darwin's theory of evolution, is another case in point. No scientific theory, whether right or wrong, affirms or denies anything taught in the Bible because the Bible doesn't address the questions which science addresses. Science teaches observable and verifiable facts about the material world and about recurring phenomena. The Bible's subject matter is different. The Bible teaches us what we need to know in order to be in right relationship with our God.

One of the most famous and harmful misunderstandings which occurred in the United States because of people's inability to separate a core teaching from an application of that teaching involved the question of slavery. As you probably know, both those who opposed slavery and those who defended it used the Bible to give authority to their arguments. Those who supported slavery used this passage from Ephesians to prove that they were right: "Slaves, obey your earthly masters with fear and trembling, in singleness of heart, as you obey Christ, not only while being watched, and in order to please them, but as slaves of Christ, doing the will of God from the heart" (Eph 6:5–6). Based on this passage slave owners convinced themselves that the order of society in which they lived, in which they owned other human beings, was God's order. It was God's will that slaves stay as slaves and obey their masters. The mistake in interpretation here is to fail to be a contextualist. In order to understand what Paul is teaching we must look at the context in which Paul was speaking. What was Paul teaching the Ephesians? Was Paul addressing the question, "Is slavery as it existed in the United States right?" Far from it. Paul was an inspired person. He came to understand that the way each of us treats every other person is the way we are treating Christ. Paul took this basic insight, his core teaching, and applied it to the social setting in which his audience lived. If a husband treated his wife as though she were Christ, how would he act? If a wife treated her husband as though he were Christ, how would she act? If parents treated children as though they were Christ, how would they act? If children treated parents as though they were Christ, how would they act? If slaves treated masters as though they were Christ, how would they act? If masters treated slaves as though they were Christ, how would they act? The passage about slaves is an application of the core truth, not the core truth itself. Paul is not addressing the question of whether or not a person should be a slave or have a slave. To use his words to give a definitive teaching about a subject which he is not addressing is to misquote him. When we misquote a biblical author what we are really doing is trying to put God's authority behind a conclusion which is not part of God's revelation. Perhaps we are trying to put biblical authority behind what we ourselves already think.

The Process of Revelation

The third context which must be considered is the context of the process of revelation. As we have already discussed, behind the Bible lie two thousand years of events, reflection upon these events, and a growing understanding of the significance of the events in the light of subsequent events. Spiritual "dawning," like the dawning of the sun, is usually gradual. People's early insights were true, but they were not the whole truth. In the light of further reflection and subsequent revelatory events, people grew in their understanding and saw more of the truth. The ramification of these facts is that we make a mistake in interpretation when we take an early insight as the fullness of revelation.

Again, an example will help to clarify the point. People who sincerely want to be faithful to the Gospel disagree on the subject of the death penalty. Some who are in favor of the death penalty quote Scripture to support their point of view: "If any harm follows, then you shall give life for life, eye for eye, tooth for tooth, hand for hand, foot for foot, burn for burn, wound for wound, stripe for stripe" (Ex 21:23–24). People use this passage to support their belief that those who take a life should lose their life. "It's right there in Scripture." This passage from Exodus reflects the understanding of right and wrong that existed in 1250 B.C. This law contains truth. It is teaching against revenge. It is saying, "If a person hurts your daughter you can't kill him in revenge." There is a sense of "fairness" behind the law, a kind of "proportionality," much as we have in our foreign policy. However, to use the passage to support the death penalty is to ignore a later insight. In Matthew's Gospel Jesus is pictured as saying, "You have heard that it was said, 'An eye for an eye and a tooth for a tooth.' But I say to you: Do not resist an evildoer" (Mt 5:38–39). Now the subject becomes more complicated. Jesus moves us beyond law to love. Jesus demands that we act for another's good, even if that other is our enemy. So, is the death penalty allowed or not? To answer the question we cannot just "proof text," that is, we cannot just quote a sentence out of context and maintain that this sentence proves that our opinion is right. We must try to understand the intent of Jesus' words in the context in which they appear, and then apply our understanding of the words to a new context. We must pray, discuss, respect, and listen to each other's opinions. We must try to respond in the love with which Jesus challenges us to act. Because revelation has been a process, and our understanding of it continues to be a process, we cannot merely "proof text" our way out of moral dilemmas. When we ignore the fact that the Bible reflects a process of revelation, we make the Bible appear to contradict itself. In addition, we harm ourselves and others. Rather than growing in the truth as a pilgrim people, we become simplistic, judgmental, and sometimes just plain wrong. To take a partial truth and present it as the whole truth is one more way to misquote the Bible.

Is Scripture a Living Word?

Can a person be a contextualist and still believe that Scripture is a living word that cuts to the marrow of the bone? The author of Hebrews says, "Indeed, the word of God is living and active, sharper than any two-edged sword, piercing until it divides soul from spirit, joints from marrow; it is able to judge the thoughts and intentions of the heart" (Heb 4:12). What does the word "word" mean here? A personification of God's word? The incarnation of God's word in Jesus Christ? The word of God in print in Scripture? Most likely the first is meant. However, it is a very common experience for those who long to hear God's word to open Scripture and experience a particular passage as a direct conversation between God's word and their heart. After having this experience, one can only think of Scripture as a living word.

Many people find it hard to integrate the idea that one must be a contextualist to understand the revelation which Scripture contains, with the idea that Scripture is a living word that speaks directly to the heart. Are the two ideas compatible? Absolutely. In fact, the two ideas are indispensable companions for people of faith. If we are contextualists who do not know that Scripture is a living word, then Scripture is in danger of becoming just one more academic subject: something we know about, but which does not speak to us in our daily lives. If we believe Scripture is a living word but are not contextualists, we have no way of knowing whether the message we are hearing is compatible with revelation or whether it is only our own selfish desires projected onto the text. Some of the most heinous crimes committed throughout history have been committed by people who believed that God told them to act as they did.

The reason I know that being a contextualist does not destroy or inhibit one's ability to hear the word as a living word is that I have often had the experience of hearing the word and being corrected by it myself. In 2 Timothy we read that "all Scripture is inspired by God and is useful for teaching, for reproof, for correction, and for training in righteousness, so that everyone who belongs to God may be proficient, equipped for every good work" (2 Tim 3:16–17). We sometimes take these words to mean that we can use the words of Scripture to reprove others. We might more fruitfully understand them if we realize that God can take the words of Scripture to reprove us. I learned this on a day when I was terribly upset because I feared that a close friend whom I trusted had lied to me. I did not know how to resolve this problem. I thought of simply asking him, but if I wasn't going to believe the answer, what good would that do? While distraught about this I happened to be reading Scripture when the words, "I know you are scrupulously honest in all moral matters" (Acts 17:22), seemed to address themselves to me. For some reason the words seemed to me to be describing my friend. I felt I was being called to love and trust rather than to doubt and judge. I acted on those words. Months later I found out that I had not been lied to at all. My friend was "scrupulously honest" and had withheld information from me in order to keep another person's confidence.

This experience caused me to ask myself, "How can we who listen to the word as a living word avoid misusing the word to support our own prejudices? How can we be sure that the living word is forming us and that we are not abusing it for our own selfish if subconscious purposes?" I think there are several things we can do to be sure of this. One is to remember that the living word heard in the depths of our own hearts will be telling us what to do, not telling us what to tell someone

---

LEVELS OF CONVERSATION

	Speaker or Writer		**Audience**
1.	Jesus spoke	to	his contemporaries— apostles, Pharisees, crowds, etc.
2.	Mark wrote	to	persecuted Christians
	Matthew wrote	to	settled Jewish Christians
	Luke wrote	to	Gentiles
	Paul wrote	to	various local churches
3.	Preaching, teaching Church through history spoke and wrote, speaks and writes	to	contemporary audiences through history
4.	God speaks	to	prayerful people

Levels three and four need to be rooted in levels one and two!

else to do. The conversation is between the living word in scripture and the living word in our heart. It is personal advice, not advice to be universalized and offered to others. Some friends do lie. It is not good advice to tell someone to always trust others. Another way we can avoid misusing the word is to talk our interpretations over with another person of faith. Where two or three are gathered in Christ's name, Christ is present. A close friend can tell us when we are rationalizing, when we are kidding ourselves. Still a third way is to be a contextualist. Whatever the living word tells us will not be incompatible with the public revelation which Scripture contains. One final and very important thing to remember is that the word, in Scripture and in our hearts, is always calling us further along the path to love. If we hear Scripture say anything to us personally which is incompatible with the call to love that the authors intend to teach, or if we take the authors' words out of context and interpret them as contrary to this call to love, we know we are misunderstanding. God is love. Scripture reveals a loving God. If we keep love as our guide we will more readily catch ourselves when we tend toward error.

"God is love. Scripture reveals a loving God." Yet we so often use Scripture to come to the opposite conclusion. Why is this? In our next section we will explore the kinds of misunderstandings and misinterpretations that have resulted in our picturing God as less than loving.

Chapter 2

Why Do We Imagine God as Angry and Punishing?

Recently I was teaching an "Introduction to Scripture" class to a group of adults from very different backgrounds. One man in the class had been raised a fundamentalist. Never once, when reading the Bible, had he considered the question, "What is the literary form of this story?" Another woman had been raised Roman Catholic but had been away from the Church for many years. She had left because she didn't like God. "He was mean."

The man was taking the Scripture course because he could see that his fundamentalist interpretation flew in the face of science. He was open to a different interpretation but struggling nevertheless. The woman was taking the course because she had come to know some very loving people who challenged her previous childhood understanding of God. She was looking for love.

I tried my best to respond to the needs of each of these adults. However, when we were discussing the story of Adam and Eve, the woman student was the one who opened everyone's eyes to the importance of being a biblical contextualist.

Later in this chapter we will do a careful interpretation of Genesis 2:4–3:24. We had just done that in class. I had explained that the story was responding to the question, "If God is all powerful and all loving, then why do human beings suffer?" The inspired author was teaching that there is a spiritual, moral order, that God has revealed this order to human beings, and that suffering inevitably results whenever people act contrary to the order. In other words, sin always causes suffering.

The man did not disagree with the idea that sin causes suffering, but he couldn't get over the fact that we were claiming that the story was not teaching history. "Are you saying this never happened?" he asked. "Are you saying the story isn't true? You're destroying Scripture."

Just as I was gearing up to explain that to say the story is not history is not to say that the story isn't true, the woman spoke from her heart.

"For me this interpretation is not destroying Scripture. It is saving it. This is the very story that made me think that God was so mean. I just didn't want to have anything to do with a God who would get so angry over one person or one couple's disobedience that he would punish the whole human race ever after. What kind of a God is that? It also made me furious that God would punish women by letting men 'lord it over them' (Gn 3:16) all their lives. Why would God do such a thing? Now I understand that the story isn't teaching anything like that. The author isn't describing what God did historically but how sin causes suffering. For a man to lord it over a woman isn't for him to follow God's order. It's just one more example the author used to show how sin is causing suffering. This story is very, very true but only if you understand that it is not history. Now I can't wait to interpret the other passages which have caused me trouble. Maybe I've misunderstood them too."

This woman's openness, honesty, enthusiasm and joy at what she was learning did more to help the man risk giving up his old understanding than anything I said to him. While I challenged his fundamentalist interpretations, her reaction assured him that to become a contextualist was not to give up faith. In fact, the exact opposite is true. To become a contextualist is to grow in faith, to trust that a deeper knowledge of Scripture leads to a deeper knowledge of God and of God's love for us. The woman found the loving God for whom she longed, and in her excitement she freed up her fellow students to risk growing with her. Both discovered that the Bible is true and that God is love.

Images

If God is love, why do we do such a good job of imagining God as less than loving? The answer to this question is very complex. However, one part of the answer is that we often misunderstand biblical images, or let others who have misunderstood biblical images preach to us or teach us. Many people understand biblical images and stories in such a way that they misunderstand the intent of the author and come away with frightening pictures of God. In this section we will first discuss "images" and the way we use them to think and talk about God, our relationship with God, and our final destiny. We will then look at passages which have been commonly misinterpreted and therefore have contributed to many people's picturing God as "mean," harsh, or frightening.

Whenever we think, talk, or write about God we are not using the concrete language of science, we are using the metaphorical language of imagery. This is not by choice but by necessity. An image is a mental picture or representation of something not present to our senses. Since God is not present to our senses, whenever we think and speak about God we must use images. Every word that we read about God in the Bible is an image. So to understand what the author intended to teach us about God we must know a little about images.

Images are comparisons. To think about or describe something not present to our senses we compare it to something which is present to our senses. So we describe God as a rock, a fortress, a shepherd, a father, a nursing mother, a warrior, a dragon, a gentle breeze, a vine, or

---

IMAGE

Definition: An image is a mental representation of something not present to the senses.

Function: An image helps us to probe a mystery; it does not give us a literal description.

---

a bridegroom. God is like each of these and like none of them. Images are not equations but comparisons. We use them not to define precisely but to probe mystery.

Depending on our age we understand images differently. Children understand images literally, as facts rather than as images. As we grow, we develop the ability to understand that an image is an image, not a fact. However, when it comes to religious imagery, many people who have the ability to understand that the vocabulary of religion is the vocabulary of imagery fail to do so. Why is this? I think some of the answer is that many people have been taught or have assumed that they shouldn't question what they learned about God as children. To do so is somehow a reflection of lack of faith or an affront to God. So they squelch "doubts" as dangerous things. Others are simply afraid to question their literal understanding of their religious images. When they question the image, they are forced to question the truth behind the image. This is often a frightening process, and while such questioning is actually a growth in faith, it is initially experienced as a crisis in faith.

Let me give an example of a concrete understanding of an image and the difficulty of growing beyond it. When I first read how one's understanding of an image is related to one's age, I decided to test out the truth of this theory. I went into an eighth grade classroom because in eighth grade the majority of students would still be young enough to be understanding images as literal statements of fact. I asked the class, "What does it mean to say that God holds you in the palm of God's hand?" Every single person in the class knew the answer to the question. It means that God is taking care of me. That is the truth behind the image. I then asked, "Does God have hands?" All but two students agreed that God does have hands. One student, however, found the question upsetting. He jumped up, pounded his desk, and said, "Of course God has hands. If God didn't have hands we couldn't be in the palm of God's hands." This young man was very bright and was just beginning to outgrow his literal understanding of the image. However, he connected the truth behind the image to his literal understanding of the image. So to give up that literal understanding was to give up the truth. This is the painful and frightening process which each of us experiences when we start to grow into adult faith. We realize that our literal understanding of images was not right. Does that mean that the truth behind the image is also not right?

Once when I was teaching this concept to a group of clergy, a Roman Catholic priest who was in the audience gave me another wonderful example. When he was in second grade he received his first communion. He was taught that he would be receiving Jesus directly into his heart. This idea was precious to him. He went to communion as often as he could and always spent time after communion thinking about how wonderful it was that Jesus was in his heart. When he reached fifth grade he was given a biology book that included pictures

---

**STEPS IN THE WAY A PERSON REGARDS IMAGES
AT VARIOUS STAGES OF FAITH DEVELOPMENT**

Age	Attitude Toward Images
Childhood	Images are understood not as images but as facts. The image and the truth behind the image are not differentiated
Late Adolescence (or any time after, depending on experience)	Images are translated into meanings. For a period of time the two remain distinct. The person may experience disillusionment or a "crisis of faith"
Sometime in Adulthood (hopefully)	Images are reunited to meaning but are no longer understood as facts. The person relinquishes the desire to be totally in control, to totally understand, and is able to probe mystery through image.

For a thorough study of faith development see James W. Fowler, *Stages of Faith: The Psychology of Human Development and the Quest for Meaning* (San Francisco: Harper and Row, 1981).

---

of the digestive tract. The very first thing he did was trace how Jesus got from his mouth to his heart. When he realized that this was impossible he felt very disillusioned. His teacher had lied. When the literal understanding of the image was shattered the truth behind the image was also threatened.

The Challenge

The challenge in this section, then, is to look at passages of Scripture that contain images of God, of our relationship with God, or of our final destiny which are often misinterpreted so that we picture God as less than loving. For each passage we will ask three questions: "What is the misunderstanding that people have in regard to this passage?" "What error in interpretation lies behind this misunderstanding?" "What is the passage actually teaching?" In order to respond to these questions we will have to be contextualists.

OLD TESTAMENT PASSAGES

1. Genesis 2:4–3:24   God punishes the whole human race

The Misunderstanding

We briefly discussed the story of the man and woman in the garden in our introduction to this section. There we named one misunderstanding which the story can cause: God seems "mean." Those who understand the story in this way ask: "Why did God punish the whole human race for the disobedient act of one couple? Isn't this unjust?" Another question which is triggered by this story is: "Why would a loving God create the 'tree of the knowledge of good and evil' in the first place? If God hadn't created the tree, Adam and Eve couldn't have eaten from it." Still another question is: "Since the fall, aren't men just acting within God's order when they lord it over women? Isn't that the 'proper place' of men and women now?" Others don't ask questions, but their failure to ask questions results in their drawing false conclusions. They try to use the story to answer questions which science, not Scripture, is able to address.

Why the Error in Interpretation?

Most of the false conclusions drawn from the story of the man and woman in the garden result from a misunderstanding of the literary form of the story. If we understand the literary form of the story, we will not misinterpret its teaching. This story does not present itself as either history or science. So to draw conclusions from the story as though we were reading history or science is to completely misunderstand the intent of the author. If we were to discuss such questions as whether or not God could make a snake talk, or whether or not the whole human race descended from a single couple, we would be discussing the "legality of left-handedness." We would be discussing topics which are not addressed by the author and which are irrelevant to revelation.

The text of the story itself informs the reader that the literary form is something other than history or science. One way in which we are "clued in" to the literary form is by the use of obvious symbols. The plot of the story includes a "tree of life" and a "tree of the knowledge of good and evil." We all know that these are not the names of trees in our neighborhood. The trees function as symbols. If you eat the fruit of the first tree you will not die. If you eat the fruit of the second tree you will come to know evil, and by contrast you will have a more self-conscious knowledge of good too: good lost.

Other details that help us identify the literary form are the descriptions of the snake and of God. The author of the story uses "personification" in describing the snake. Personification is a literary technique which attributes to things that are not human the attributes of a human. Snakes don't talk. They never did. When an author pictures a snake or any other animal as talking, the author is not trying to claim that on this one occasion God worked a miracle and made a snake talk. Rather the author is informing us about the literary form of the story. The talking snake is an image. It symbolizes temptation.

The description of God is "anthropomorphic." This too is a literary technique. To describe God "anthropomorphically" is to describe God as though God were a human being. In this story God is not all-knowing. When God realizes that the man should not be alone, God creates a number of animals as companions that don't "fill the bill." After the man and woman sin, God knows nothing about it. God comes for a nightly walk and talk. God learns that something has gone wrong when the man hides because he is naked.

The very way in which the author tells the story lets us know that we are reading a symbol story, not a literal account of historical events. Without even knowing the name of the literary form we are, nevertheless, directed by the text to interpret the story as symbolic rather than as historical.

The Teaching

The story of the man and woman in the garden teaches us that sin always causes suffering. We will now look at the plot of the story and at the author's use of symbols to see how this teaching is accomplished.

If one were to summarize the plot of this story one might say: "God made a place of no suffering and put the man and woman in it. God explained the 'rules.' The man and the woman were disobedient. After that their life was full of suffering."

The symbols in the story are very rich. The man represents each of us. What is true of the man is true of every human being. Before the man disobeys God all of his relationships are good: his relationship with self (he is naked but not ashamed), his relationship with the other person whom he needs in order to love and be loved, his relationship with God (God comes to walk and talk each evening), and his relationship with his environment.

The man also has the security of knowing what he may and may not do because God has revealed the "order" in the garden to him. This order, symbolized by the presence of the trees from which the man may eat and the one from which he may not eat, represents the fact that there is right and wrong. God has explained to the man that he must not do what is wrong, because if he does, on the day that he does, he will die. This plot detail makes the real subject of the story obvious. The story is not about physical life and death but about spiritual life and death. The man does not die physically on the day that he disobeys, but he does die spiritually. He disrupts all of his relationships: with self (he is now ashamed of his nakedness), with the other (he blames rather than loves), with God (he hides), and with the environment (he will have to work by the sweat of his brow). The "sin" is not specific. "Eating" is a good symbol for sin because eating is something we choose to do, just as sin is. Also, what we eat becomes a part of us. Sin also becomes a part of us. We can be forgiven for our sin, but we are a different person afterward. The difference is described in the name of the tree: we now have a knowledge of good and evil which we lacked before.

The source of this story rests not in an individual event but in a universal human experience, a mysterious reality, the reality of human

INTERPRETING A MYTH

Through concrete symbols and a concrete plot the author speaks about what is beyond comprehension.

Adam	Each person—all of us
Eve	The other person whom we need to love and by whom we need to be loved
Garden	A place of no suffering
God's instructions	Moral and spiritual order
Tree of knowledge of good and evil	The possibility of acting contrary to the spiritual order
Tree of life	Avoid physical death—one kind of suffering
Naked but unashamed	Self-acceptance
Serpent	Temptation
Eating	Sin
Naked but ashamed	Self-alienation
Hiding	Loss of capacity to respond to God's love
Punishment	Suffering, known from experience, which is seen as the natural consequence of disobeying the spiritual order
Expelled from garden and unable to return	Human beings are powerless to undo the effects of sin
PLOT:	No suffering—sin—suffering
THEME:	Sin always causes suffering

suffering. The author wonders why human beings suffer if God really is all powerful and all loving. The inspired author comes to a partial answer: sin causes suffering. There is a spiritual order which has been revealed. When human beings act contrary to that order they inevitably bring suffering on themselves and on everyone else because they become less capable of love. The "punishments" placed on God's lips are not so much punishments as they are ramifications. The author pictures God explaining the ramifications of their behavior to the man and woman. However, God does not withdraw God's love. God tries to help the man and woman by making garments for them.

That the story is about each of us is evident in the names given the man and woman. "Adam" is not a masculine, singular noun but a collective noun. "Eve" means "the mother of all the living." The story is about the human condition. We bring a great deal of suffering on ourselves because we chose to sin. Whether or not we "get caught" is irrelevant. Sin makes us less capable of love and so destroys our self-respect and our loving relationships.

A contextualist who asks the question "What is the literary form of this story?" would name the form "myth." A "myth" is an imaginative and symbolic story about a reality beyond our comprehension. The function of a myth is to orient us in a moral universe. This use of the word "myth" needs to be distinguished from the frequent use of the word "myth" to mean "something we once believed to be true but now know is false." We are using the word "myth" to name a form, not to comment on the truth or falsity of the content of the story.

The reason this "myth" is in the canon is because the lesson which the story teaches, the intent of the author, is true. Sin does cause suffering. Sin is never the better choice. The inspired author was very insightful, but the author's answer to the question regarding the cause of suffering is a partial answer. However, for hundreds of years the answer was understood to be the whole answer. For centuries people believed that all suffering was due to sin. So the true, but partial, answer which this author taught must be understood in the context of the two thousand year process of revelation. This story does not represent all that Scripture has to teach on the subject of suffering. Nonetheless, what the story does teach is true.

2. Genesis 19:24–26   Lot's wife is turned into a pillar of salt

The Misunderstanding

Many people find the story of Sodom and Gomorrah terribly frightening. Not only does it appear to picture God as one who, when filled with anger, will destroy everyone in a town except for God's favorites (Lot and Lot's family), but it also pictures God as turning Lot's wife into a pillar of salt for a very slight misdemeanor: looking back as she flees a catastrophic event in her town. "Then the Lord rained on Sodom and Gomorrah sulfur and fire from the Lord out of heaven, and he overthrew those cities, and all the Plain, and all the inhabitants of the cities, and what grew on the ground. But Lot's wife, behind him, looked back, and she became a pillar of salt" (Gn 19:24–26).

Is this passage teaching us to fear God because something similar might happen to us? In the New Testament the destruction of Sodom and Gomorrah is referred to as the image of a terrible end. When Jesus describes the judgment rendered toward towns that reject the disciples Jesus is pictured as saying, "Amen, I say to you, it will be more tolerable for the land of Sodom and Gomorrah on the day of judgment than for that town" (Mt 10:15).

Why the Error in Interpretation?

Again the primary source of error here is a misunderstanding of the literary form, although the presence of some "beliefs of the time" also plays a role.

The literary form of this story, and of many of the stories in the book of Genesis, is "legend." A legend is an imaginative and symbolic story that has an historical core. I'm sure you are familiar with legends, such as the one about George Washington and the cherry tree. You probably have family legends too. Think about occasions when your family gathers together on holidays. Stories are told, some about relatives who have died, others about "the days of our youth." Some stories are told every year, and they get better with each telling. The intent of the storyteller is not to recreate events exactly as they occurred, but to "build up" a certain characteristic which a person had or to teach the younger members of the family about some of the virtues and foibles of fellow family members so that they might emulate or avoid those same characteristics.

Legends which are told from generation to generation, as were the legends in Genesis, are not claiming exact quotations when they report a person in direct conversation with God. This is a literary technique. The story-teller is "allowed" to be a good story-teller. The story-teller may add imaginative details that support the point of the story. The story-teller may also make the story more applicable or more interesting to the immediate audience by adding details of setting or application that are contemporary with the generation of the story-teller's audience rather than with the generation of the people about whom the story is being told.

Legends often include "etiologies." That is, they include an explanation for how something known to the story-teller and the audience came to be the way it is. Say that both author and audience were aware of the name of a town, or a derogatory expression, or a strangely shaped rock formation. The story-teller might include an imaginative explanation of how this name, or expression, or rock formation came into existence, thus making the story more immediate for the audience and giving the events in the story some concrete expression in the lives of the listeners.

Legends also include presumptions of the time. The story is not told to teach these presumptions. The presumptions are just included as the story goes along.

One presumption of the time during which the Genesis legends developed was that all suffering was due to sin. This presumption led people to interpret natural disasters, such as earthquakes, as God's punishment. We hear this presumption behind the story of the destruction of Sodom and Gomorrah. The fact that the town was destroyed must be because God was punishing the inhabitants. While it is true that sin causes suffering, it is also true that not all suffering is caused by sin. We learn this at a later stage of revelation than is represented by some of the stories in Genesis. We will discuss this later insight further when we discuss passages in the book of Job. However, for those who told and retold the legends in Genesis, the presumption was that since the

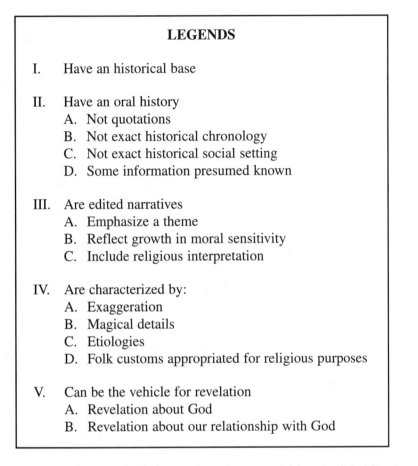

LEGENDS

I.   Have an historical base

II.   Have an oral history
    A. Not quotations
    B. Not exact historical chronology
    C. Not exact historical social setting
    D. Some information presumed known

III.   Are edited narratives
    A. Emphasize a theme
    B. Reflect growth in moral sensitivity
    C. Include religious interpretation

IV.   Are characterized by:
    A. Exaggeration
    B. Magical details
    C. Etiologies
    D. Folk customs appropriated for religious purposes

V.   Can be the vehicle for revelation
    A. Revelation about God
    B. Revelation about our relationship with God

towns were destroyed, God must have been punishing the inhabitants of the town.

The Teaching

The teachings in the story of the destruction of Sodom and Gomorrah must be distinguished from the presumptions made by the author. The teachings are that God is always faithful to God's promises, and that one must be wholehearted in one's response to God's love.

First, God's fidelity. This story, in which Lot and his family are saved from destruction, is part of a series of stories that revolve around

God's covenant promise to Abraham: "I will make of you a great nation, and I will bless you; I will make your name great so that you will be a blessing. I will bless those who bless you and curse those who curse you. All the communities of the earth shall find blessing in you" (Gn 12:2). This passage itself needs some explanation. Remember, we are not reading a quotation from God. God is pictured anthropomorphically, blessing and cursing as humans did at the time. Remember, too, another presumption of the time was that God loved Israel more than God loved other nations, a belief that was held until after the Babylonian exile (587 B.C.–537 B.C.). The point of this passage is that God entered into a relationship of mutual love with God's people.

The stories about Lot are part of this series of stories because Lot is a relative of Abraham's; Lot is Abraham's nephew. The stories are about God's fidelity to God's promises. The author explicitly states that this is the purpose of the stories: "Thus it came to pass; when God destroyed the Cities of the Plain, he was mindful of Abraham by sending Lot away from the upheaval by which God overthrew the cities where Lot had been living" (Gn 19:29). So instead of intending to instill fear about God's horrible punishments, the story is intended to instill awe at God's gracious fidelity to God's promises.

The sentence about Lot's wife being turned into a pillar of salt is an etiological detail intended to teach the importance of single-heartedness. There was, most likely, some rock formation that looked like a woman turning back. By including this etiological detail of the source of the rock formation, the story-teller provided the audience of the time with a visible reminder of the lesson to be learned: When one is in a covenant relationship of love with God, one has no need ever to look back. To look back is to "atrophy." Jesus is pictured as teaching much the same idea in the New Testament when he says, "No one who sets a hand to the plow and looks to what was left behind is fit for the kingdom of God" (Lk 9:62).

Even though the destruction of Sodom and Gomorrah can be used as an image of a terrible end, the intent of the story in Genesis is not to threaten destruction or to cause people to fear God's punishment. To use the story to teach such lessons is to misinterpret it. Rather, the intent of the story is to teach good news: God is always faithful to God's promises.

3. Deuteronomy 7:1–11   Kill the women and children

The Misunderstanding

Those of us who claim to be Christians have, through the course of history, sometimes treated our enemies as though they were God's enemies. We have acted as though God loves us and hates those of other nations or religions. A passage which might feed such hate if it were misinterpreted is: "…and when the Lord your God gives them (i.e. other nations) over to you and you defeat them, then you must utterly destroy them. Make no covenant with them and show them no mercy…" (Dt 7:2). Does this passage require us to destroy our enemies, to show them no mercy?

Why the Error in Interpretation?

The error in interpreting this passage results from failure to consider two important contexts: the context of the beliefs of the time, and the context of the process of revelation. When we say that the Bible contains a two thousand year process of revelation we are saying that early understandings and stories do not represent the fullness of truth which the whole two thousand year process, the whole Bible, represents. At the time that this passage took form, the inspired author did not know something that the nation Israel learned after the Babylonian Exile: that God loves other nations too. Israel learned this truth because a later inspired author, the author of the book of Jonah, reflected on the way in which God saved the Israelites from exile. When God saved them, God did it, as expected, by sending a "messiah," a chosen person who defeated the nation's political enemies and freed the people from foreign oppression. However, completely against all expectation, the chosen messiah was not an Israelite, but a Persian, who defeated the Babylonians and let the Israelites return to the holy land. The author of Jonah, reflecting on the significance of this event, realized that God must love other nations. Otherwise God would not have chosen a person from another nation to be God's saving instrument. But until this event had occurred, the Israelites did not understand that God loved other nations too.

The Teaching

Even given this "belief of the time," that God did not love other nations, what good could possibly have been taught by a passage such as this? The Deuteronomic editor lived at a time of reform under King Josiah (640-609 B.C.). He was trying to teach the people to renew their covenant commitment to Yahweh, and to express this renewed commitment by obedience to the law. He interpreted the destruction of the Northern Kingdom by the Assyrians (722 B.C.) as being the result of lack of obedience to covenant love, the result of lack of obedience to the law. He wanted his audience to obey the law and to recognize that they were privileged to have been chosen by God to enter into this covenant relationship, so he threatened them with similar destruction themselves if they were not obedient. "It was not because you were more numerous than any other people that the Lord set his heart on you and chose you—for you were the fewest of all peoples. It was because the Lord loved you and kept the oath that he swore to your ancestors, that the Lord has brought you out with a mighty hand, and redeemed you from the house of slavery, from the hand of Pharaoh king of Egypt. Know therefore that the Lord your God is God, the faithful God who maintains covenant loyalty with those who love him and keep his commandments, to a thousand generations, and who repays in their own person those who reject him....Therefore, observe diligently the commandment—the statutes, and the ordinances—that I am commanding you today" (Dt 7:7–9, 11).

Again, the teaching is about God's love and fidelity toward Israel, and about the inevitable suffering which Israel's infidelity will bring about. That a belief of the time, a belief that the nation is justified in destroying its enemies, is placed on God's lips does not give us permission to hate or destroy our enemies on the assumption that our enemies are God's enemies too. Israel grew beyond this assumption several hundred years after this passage was written. Therefore, to use the passage to support such thinking is to misinterpret it. Jesus fulfilled the revelation about our attitude toward our enemies when he taught, "You have heard that it was said, 'You shall love your neighbor and hate your enemy.' But I say to you, Love your enemies and pray for those who persecute you, so that you may be children of your Father in heaven, for he makes his sun rise on the evil and on the good, and sends rain on the righteous and on the unrighteous" (Mt 5:43–45). In the light of these words we have no excuse for maintaining a belief that we are doing good when we destroy an enemy.

4. Job 1:1–2:13   God gives Satan permission to harm Job

The Misunderstanding

Another Old Testament passage which is often misunderstood is the beginning of the book of Job in which God and Satan are pictured as arguing over whether or not Job's love of God is based on self-interest. Satan is pictured as taunting God: "Does Job fear God for nothing? Have you not put a fence around him and his house and all that he has, on every side? You have blessed the work of his hands, and his possessions have increased in the land. But stretch out your hand now, and touch all that he has, and he will curse you to your face" (Jb 1:9–11). In response to this taunt God gives Satan permission to harm Job. Does this mean that God, on occasion, agrees to give Satan power over human beings? Might the twentieth century be a time when God has given Satan power over the earth? Some people, unfortunately, not only believe that God would do this, but that God has done this. What is this passage in Job actually teaching? Does it support such a belief?

Why the Error in Interpretation?

The scene pictured in the introduction to the book of Job is easily misunderstood if one misunderstands the literary form of the passage in which the quotation appears or if one misunderstands the meaning of the word "Satan."

The book of Job is not an account of an historic event. Rather than report an event, the author wants to challenge a generally held belief:

the belief that all suffering is punishment for sin. The author of Job has observed enough of life to lead him to disagree with the generally held belief that all suffering is deserved. Not only does the author of Job disagree with this commonly held belief, but he thinks to hold such a belief is to picture God as far less loving than God actually is. When you look around at the kind of suffering which people endure, you can only come to the conclusion that if God is handing out this suffering as punishment for sin then God must not be loving. The punishment exceeds the crime. The author is having a difficult time teaching his insight because those who disagree with him think that he is challenging God's power. If God is not handing out people's suffering as well-deserved punishment, then why are people suffering? Is it because God is not all powerful? Of course God is all powerful, so the suffering must be deserved.

In order to argue his case the author of the book of Job presents a debate in which all sides of the question are argued through the appearance of various characters. The author frames the debate with an old legend which suggests that the reason for suffering is to test a person's virtue. The passage we quoted is from the beginning of this legend frame. The function of the first part of the frame is to set the stage for the debate. The frame establishes the facts that Job is innocent (God says so), and that Job is suffering.

The frame is a legend because it is an imaginative and symbolic story with an historical core: a person named Job, known for his virtue, was an historical person at the time of the patriarchs. However, the old legend is not meant to teach something about Job, but to teach something about the purpose of suffering. Job is the character around whom the legend grew because of his reputation for goodness. The legend in its present setting functions, not to describe an actual event, but to set the stage for the debate which will follow.

In order to understand the author's intent in this story one must understand not only the literary form, but also what the word "Satan" meant to the contemporary audience. If we presume that the word "Satan" meant to the original audience what it means to us, that the word refers to the devil, we will make a second error in interpretation. As the story makes clear, the word "Satan" is not referring to a devil, but to one of the "heavenly beings" (see Jb 1:6) who is part of God's heavenly court. God engages Satan in conversation and lets Satan test out Satan's theory that Job is not as virtuous as he appears. Satan might be compared to a prosecuting attorney in the heavenly court. He is not pictured as an evil being in the book of Job.

The Teaching

The teaching in the book of Job comes from the interaction between the debate and its legend frame. To learn the author's intent one must read the whole book. In the debate Job's friends argue that Job must have sinned or he would not be suffering. However, because of the legend frame, the reading audience knows that Job's friends are wrong. Job is not suffering because he has sinned. God has established Job's innocence. At the end of the debate God appears and addresses the

---

STRUCTURE OF DEBATE IN THE BOOK OF JOB

Eliphaz's Three Speeches
Chapters 4–5
Chapters 15
Chapters 22

Job's Responses
Chapters 6–7
Chapters 16–17
Chapters 23–24

Bildad's Three Speeches
Chapter 8
Chapter 18
25:1–6; 26:5–14

Job's Responses
Chapters 9–10
Chapter 19
26:1–4; 27:1–12

Zophar's Three Speeches
Chapter 11
Chapter 20
24:18–24?; 27:13–23?

Job's Responses
Chapters 12–14
Chapters 21
Chapters 29–31

The debate consists of three cycles of arguments. The third cycle presents problems and various attempts have been made to reconstruct it. Chapters 32–37 are Elihu's rebuke of Job.

question which is on the author's mind: "Why is an innocent person suffering?"

While a total answer to the question is beyond the author's comprehension, he nevertheless pictures God explaining, through a variety of questions and statements, that suffering sometimes has a purpose other than punishment. As the story comes to a close with the second half of the legend frame, God is pictured as praising Job and blaming Job's friends for saying things about God that are not true (see Jb 42:7b). Attributing all suffering to a punishing God does not protect God's reputation. It destroys it. Such a conclusion implies that God is unloving. The book teaches that not all suffering is due to sin. Although the purpose of suffering was still beyond the inspired author's understanding, the author at least was able to teach that suffering had a purpose other than punishment. Not until the innocent Jesus Christ suffered and rose from the dead did we learn about the redemptive power of suffering.

There are other Old Testament passages, some in the works of the prophets, which have caused people to imagine God as unloving. We will address those passages in Chapter 3 of this book when we discuss the role of a prophet, and, in that context, the book of Revelation. For now, let us move on to New Testament passages which are commonly misinterpreted to portray God as unloving. We will see how these misinterpretations cause people not to hear the "good news" which the passages actually proclaim.

NEW TESTAMENT PASSAGES

The Gospels definitely teach that we as human beings are and will be held accountable for our actions, and that the fate of those who do good and those who do evil is not the same. Are the facts of judgment and punishment good news or bad news? In apocalyptic literature the message of judgment and punishment is good news. Apocalyptic literature, such as the book of Daniel and the book of Revelation, is written to offer hope to people who are facing persecution. Therefore, the message of judgment and punishment is good news in these books because it is assuring the victims of persecution that their oppressors will not prevail, but will be judged and punished by God. We will discuss passages of judgment and punishment in the book of Revelation in our next chapter. However, there are other passages of judgment and punishment in the New Testament. The Synoptic Gospels, that is, Mark's, Matthew's and Luke's Gospels, also threaten severe punishment for those who choose sin. We will now examine a number of passages from the Gospels which deal with judgment and punishment to see if these passages give us reason to conclude that God is less than loving.

5. Matthew 5:22   Hell

The Misunderstanding

In "the sermon on the mount" Jesus is pictured as saying, "You have heard that it was said to those of ancient times, 'You shall not murder': and 'Whoever murders shall be liable to judgment.' But I say to you that if you are angry with a brother or sister, you will be liable to judgment; and if you insult a brother or sister, you will be liable to the council; and if you say, 'You fool,' you will be liable to the hell of fire..." (Mt 5:21–22). This passage is one of many in which Jesus is pictured as referring to a place of punishment called "hell," "the abyss," "Hades," "the pit," "Gehenna," "eternal fire," or simply a place of "eternal punishment" (see Mt 5:29, 30; 18:9; Mk 9:43, 47; Lk 12:5). These references have been understood very concretely by many. As a result, they have concluded that a punishing God, as part of the order of creation, has prepared a place of eternal, fiery torture for those who "die in sin." The slightest infraction, such as calling another person a fool, could inflame God's ire and result in God condemning someone to eternal punishment. Those who hold this belief live in fear.

Why the Error in Interpretation?

This error in interpretation results from understanding an image as a literal fact rather than as a tool with which to describe things that are beyond our knowledge. We use images to probe mystery, not to describe literally that to which we are referring. The image "Gehenna"

STEPS IN THE DEVELOPMENT OF
THE IDEA OF "GEHENNA" OR HELL

- Gehenna was the name of a valley that divided Jerusalem from the hills to the south and west. The valley was most likely named after its owner. It is also called the valley of Hennon, or the valley of the sons of Hennon. Originally the word had no negative connotations.

- Gehenna became the site of a cultic shrine where human sacrifice was practiced. The valley became associated with fire and abomination.

- Jeremiah warns that the valley will be the site of unburied bodies when the city of Jerusalem is destroyed (Jer 7:32–33).

- Isaiah warns that the valley will be the site of the dead bodies of those who have rebelled against Yahweh (Is 66:24). Isaiah's imagery is used in Mk 9:48.

- The images associated with Gehenna are attributed to Sheol. Sheol was originally not a place of punishment, just the place of the dead. Sheol becomes a place of unending fire, darkness, and corruption.

- Jesus use the imagery of his time when he describes what happens to sinners (Mt 5:22).

- The same truths can be taught without using this imagery (Rom 2:5–1).

---

grew out of the Israelites' experience of horrible events. Originally the word did not have negative connotations. It referred simply to the valley that divides Jerusalem from the hills to the south and west. Scripture scholars surmise that the name Gehenna is probably the name of an owner of the property. It is also referred to as the valley of Hennon, or the valley of the sons of Hennon. However, as time passed, the word became associated with abominations and fire because it was the site of a cultic shrine where human sacrifice was practiced (see Jer 32:35). In the book of Jeremiah the prophet warns the inhabitants of Judah (the southern kingdom) that when Jerusalem is destroyed the valley will be so full of the dead bodies of those killed trying to defend the city that there will not be enough room to bury the corpses. "Therefore, the days are surely coming, says the Lord, when it will no more be called Topheth, or the valley of the son of Hinnom, but the valley of Slaughter; for they will bury in Topheth until there is no more room. The corpses of this people will be food for the birds of the air, and for the animals of the earth; and no one will frighten them away" (Jer 7:32–33).

Isaiah adds to the imagery used to describe this horrible place. Isaiah describes the fate of those who rebel against God and so are excluded from the saving acts which God will perform on Jerusalem's behalf. To those who are faithful Yahweh is pictured as saying, "As a mother comforts her child, so I will comfort you; you shall be comforted in Jerusalem" (Is 66:13). Those who are saved "will go out and look at the dead bodies of the people who have rebelled against me; for their worm shall not die, their fire shall not be quenched, and they shall be an abhorrence to all flesh" (Is 66:24). Some of Isaiah's imagery is later used in the New Testament to describe a place of eternal punishment (see Mk 9:48).

As time passed, then, Gehenna was no longer thought of as a geographical place but became associated with Sheol, the place of the dead. Originally Sheol was not seen as a place of punishment, but as the place where everyone goes at death. However, by the time Jesus lived the images associated with Gehenna were attributed to Sheol: unending fire, darkness, and corruption. Jesus is pictured as using the imagery of his time when he describes what happens to sinners.

Later New Testament writers teach the same truths of judgment and punishment without the same imagery. For instance, Paul teaches the same truths when he says, "But by your hard and impenitent heart you are storing up wrath for yourself on the day of wrath, when God's righteous judgment will be revealed. For he will repay according to each one's deeds: to those who by patiently doing good seek for glory and honor and immortality, he will give eternal life; while for those who are self-seeking and who obey not the truth but wickedness, there will be wrath and fury. There will be anguish and distress for everyone who does evil, the Jew first and also the Greek, but glory and honor and peace for everyone who does good, the Jew first and also the Greek" (Rom 2:5–10). Paul does not use the same images Jesus used because Paul is writing to Romans. The images associated with Gehenna would not have the same meaning for a Gentile audience.

The Teaching

The intent behind Jesus' statement, "If you say, 'you fool,' you will be liable to the hell of fire" (Mt 5:22), is not to give a literal description of the fate of those who choose sin, but to teach the crowd that right relationship with God, the only road to happiness, is integrally connected to right relationship with each other. That is why Jesus goes on to say, "So when you are offering your gift at the altar, if you remember that your brother or sister has something against you, leave your gift there before the altar and go; first be reconciled to your brother or sister, and then come and offer your gift" (Mt 5:23–24).

In the sermon on the mount Jesus is presented as the new Moses, as the one who has authority from God to teach the new law. The new law does not undo the old law; it "fulfills" or extends it. The old law was good. It moved people away from hate and toward love. However, it did not go far enough. Jesus demands much more from his disciples than did the old law. True, Jesus' disciples still must obey the old law in that they "shall not kill." But that law doesn't begin to demand what Jesus demands. Jesus demands that we treat every other person with love, that we always act for the other's good. If we choose the path of love we will build up God's kingdom and live eternally in a loving relationship with God and others. If we choose hate we will be excluded from the loving relationship which God wishes us to have with God and with each other. The details of how we will experience that exclusion are unknown to us. We can speak of the details of our afterlife only through images.

6. Mark 9:43   Abuse of self and others (see also Mt 5:30)

The Misunderstanding

In nineteenth century England the punishment for shoplifting was to cut off the person's hand—this in a Christian country. Not too long ago I read a story about a woman in our own United States of America who killed her daughter because her daughter had become involved in prostitution. The woman thought she was "saving" her daughter. An isolated act by one unbalanced person? Perhaps, but it is also true that many people who behave in cruel and abusive ways justify their behavior in their own minds by thinking that it is "better" for someone to receive this treatment, and hopefully learn a lesson, than to "go to hell." Was Jesus really recommending self mutilation or the physical abuse of others as a path to spiritual wholeness? Many people think that he was, and so they treat others and/or themselves with an unhealthy harshness rather than with love.

Why the Error in Interpretation?

Those who interpret Jesus' words as calling for such harsh behavior as cutting off one's hand fail to understand the words in the context of the conversation in which they occur. In Mark, Jesus is pictured as saying these words to his disciples immediately after they exhibit two faults which are blocks to holiness: the desire to be considered "great" in the eyes of others (see Mk 9:33–37), and the tendency to distrust, and perhaps obstruct, the good actions of a person who is not part of our "group" (see Mk 9:38–39). In Matthew, Jesus is pictured as saying these words as part of the sermon on the mount, right after he has taught that a person who so much as looks at a woman with lust has committed adultery with her in his heart (see Mt 5:28). In neither Gospel is Jesus pictured as meaning his words literally. He is trying to get his listeners to react defensively to his words so that they will arrive at the very truth which he has been trying to teach. He wants to get his listeners to understand that discipleship and holiness are internal matters, not merely external matters.

The Teaching

Jesus' statement begins with the word "if." "If your hand causes you to sin." No one's hand causes him or her to sin. Nor does one's eye, or one's foot. It would be possible to lose your eyes, your hands, and your feet and still sin. This is true because sin is a matter of the heart, not of the hand. Jesus has a very hard time teaching this lesson. His audience, raised to believe that obedience to the law constitutes holiness, while disobedience to the law constitutes sin, thinks of sin as something external rather than as something internal. In fact, holiness is not merely refraining from sinful action. Rather, holiness has to do with the love in one's heart. In order to try to teach this lesson to an audience who is having difficulty hearing it, Jesus as much as says, "Well, if it is really your hand that is causing you to sin, you could solve the problem by cutting it off. Why don't you do that? To lose a hand is certainly less serious than to lose your loving relationship with God and others." The expected reaction is, "We can't cut off our hands! That would be a terrible thing to do! And besides, it isn't really our hands that cause us to sin in the first place. We could still long for worldly honor and lust after others in our hearts whether we have our hands or not. The only way to avoid sin is to change what is in our hearts." Jesus' response to this might well be, "Ah! Now you see my point!" Holiness does not rest in cutting off our hands, or even in washing our hands, as the law prescribed. Rather, holiness rests in conversion of heart. We need to learn how to love. Then we won't even be thinking about worldly honor or about abusing another for our own physical pleasure. We will be thinking about how to act for the other's good instead.

7. Luke 9:60   Neglect of family responsibilities (see also Mt 8:22)

The Misunderstanding

In both Matthew's and Luke's Gospels Jesus is pictured as saying, "Let the dead bury their own dead," to a man who has responded to Jesus' invitation to follow him with the words, "Lord, first let me go and bury my father" (Lk 9:59; Mt 8:21). In Luke the interchange is followed by another in which a person says to Jesus, " 'I will follow you, Lord; but let me first say farewell to those at my home.' Jesus said to him, 'No one who puts a hand to the plow and looks back is fit for the kingdom of God' " (Lk 9:61–62). Is Jesus teaching that true discipleship necessarily involves freeing oneself from family responsibilities? Can adult children ignore the needs of their elderly parents and chalk it up to discipleship? For many years this passage was interpreted in just this way. I once had a conversation with a woman religious who was in her eighties. She told me that when she left for the convent at the age of fourteen she refused to turn and wave goodbye to her parents because she had "put her hand to the plow" and thought it would be wrong to look back. For many years religious orders would not give their members permission to return home, even to tend to the needs of a dying parent in his or her last days. Is this really what Jesus is asking of us?

Why the Error in Interpretation?

Again, the error in interpretation occurs when one fails to distinguish between the literal meaning of the words and the intentional meaning of the words. Those who interpret these words literally support their interpretation with other passages which they misinterpret in the same way, such as passages that picture James and John, the sons of Zebedee, deserting their father on the spot at the call of Jesus (see Mk 1:19–20; Mt 4:21–22; Lk 5:10–11), or passages that teach that we may not ignore our responsibilities as disciples by acting as though our only responsibilities are to our families (see Mt 10:35, 37; Mk 10:29–30; Lk 12:53; 14:26). Those who misinterpret these passages also ignore another passage which explicitly states that one cannot justify the neglect of one's parents in the name of religious duty. In this passage the Pharisees have asked Jesus why his disciples break "the tradition of the elders" by failing to wash their hands before they eat. Jesus responds, "And why do you break the commandment of God for the sake of your tradition? For God said, 'Honor your father and your mother,' and, 'Whoever speaks evil of father or mother must surely die.' But you say that whoever tells father or mother, 'Whatever support you might have had from me is given to God,' then that person need not honor the father. So, for the sake of your tradition, you make void the word of God. You hyp-ocrites!" (Mt 15:3–7; see also Mk 7:9–13). This passage directly attacks the misinterpretation. But what did Jesus mean when he told the man to "leave the dead to bury the dead"?

The Teaching

In both Matthew's and Luke's Gospels the question behind the "leave the dead to bury the dead" passage is, "What is involved in dis-cipleship?" In each Gospel the conversation between Jesus and the man who says he wants to "bury his father" is preceded by a conver-sation with a man who says, "I will follow you wherever you go." Jesus responds, "Foxes have holes, and birds of the air have nests; but the Son of Man has nowhere to lay his head" (Lk 9:57–58; see also Mt 8:18–19). This man is too quick to embrace discipleship. He has not considered the ramifications of the choice. Once one becomes a disci-ple, being faithful to discipleship must be the top priority in one's life. Hardships will follow, and one must be prepared to accept them. Discipleship is not "settling down for life." Rather, it is a constant jour-ney of trying to discern and respond in love to God's will. The second man, who wants to "bury" his father, acts as though he is willing to fol-low Jesus, but not today. He does not claim that his father is dead, only that he wants to postpone answering Jesus' call until his father actually dies, which may be years and years. This interpretation is supported by the fact that nowhere else in the Gospels does Jesus fail to react with compassion when a person is grieving over the actual death of a loved one (see Lk 7:12; Jn 11:33). Jesus is not being rude and unfeeling in the face of someone's heartfelt grief. Rather, Jesus is responding to a procrastinator whose "Yes, but…" means "no."

The interchange between Jesus and the person who wants to return home to say goodbye to his family, as well as the story of the calling of the sons of Zebedee, reinforce the lesson. Discipleship must be a wholehearted response to God's love. While other responsibilities do not evaporate, they nevertheless take second place to one's commit-ment to God. We cannot use our families as an excuse for refusing to follow Christ, nor can we use Christ as an excuse for failing to act lov-ingly toward our family. A true disciple of Christ will "honor his father and his mother," but will not let father, mother, or any other family bond take priority over fidelity to God.

8. Matthew 25:41   Eternal punishment

The Misunderstanding

Matthew 25:31–46 is often called "the parable of the judgment of the nations." In it, Jesus tells his disciples a story in which the "Son of Man" comes in his glory and judges all the nations who are gathered before him. Those who have been attentive and responsive to the needs of others inherit "the kingdom." Those who have failed to be attentive and responsive to the needs of others are sent to eternal punishment.

Those who misinterpret the parable of the judgment of the nations use the parable to draw conclusions on subjects which the parable is not addressing. The parable is not teaching the answer to the question, "Exactly what is hell like? If you are sent there are you there forever?" We cannot use this parable to prove that God sends people to eternal damnation. Nor is the parable responding to the question, "In order for an act of kindness to be spiritually beneficial, must one be self-consciously doing it for Christ?" Some people use the parable to address this question because those who are commended for their good works seem unaware that they have ever seen "the king" hungry, thirsty, or naked. Nor is the parable about the relationship between non-Christians (i.e. "Gentiles") and Christians. When the king says, "…just as you did it for one of the least of these who are members of my family, you did it to me" (Mt 25:40), we are not being taught that other nations will be judged by the way they treat Christians. Rather, the parable is teaching the disciples that the way they treat others, especially those most in need, will determine whether or not they enter the kingdom.

Why the Error in Interpretation?

The parable of the judgment of the nations is often misinterpreted because it is not recognized as a parable. Instead it is treated as though it were an allegory. In order to explain how this mistake can sometimes lead to errors in interpretation, it is necessary to explain the difference between a parable and an allegory.

A parable is a story whose function is to correct and call to conversion the audience to whom the story is told. The parable accomplishes its function because the audience is compared to someone or something in the story. The lesson of the parable derives from the comparison. So in order to know what is being taught through a parable, we need to ask ourselves several questions:

1. To whom is Jesus speaking?
2. What precipitated Jesus' story? A parable is always the middle of a conversation. To know what the parable is teaching, we have to put it in the context of the conversation that has already occurred between Jesus and those to whom he is telling the story.
3. With whom or what in the story does the audience compare?
4. Based on this comparison, what is Jesus teaching his specific audience?

The lesson of a parable is a single lesson based on a single comparison.

An allegory, on the other hand, is not based on a single comparison but on a number of comparisons. In an allegory there are two levels of meaning: the literal level, that is, the literal meaning of the words, and the intentional level, that is, the level of meaning derived from the comparisons. The teaching is always drawn from the intentional level, not from the literal level.

An example will help to illustrate this point. In Luke's Gospel Jesus tells a parable about an unjust judge who feared neither God nor man and a widow who kept pestering and pestering him until he gave her what she wanted (see Lk 18:1–5). The narrator's voice tells us that "Jesus told them (i.e. the disciples) a parable about their need to pray always and not to lose heart" (Lk 18:1). So the Gospel itself tells us that this is a parable, not an allegory, and that it is intended to teach the disciples to pray constantly. However, if the Gospel did not tell us this we could still figure it out for ourselves if we knew how to interpret a parable. In the passage, the disciples compare to the widow because they too need something that another has the power to grant. The lesson to be learned is drawn from that comparison. Just as the widow benefited

---

INTERPRETING
PARABLES AND ALLEGORIES

A Parable: Look for the one basic comparison between an element in the story and the audience listening to the story. The lesson comes from this comparison. Ask yourself:
- To whom is Jesus speaking?
- What's the topic?
- With what person or thing in the story does the audience compare?
- What lesson is drawn from this comparison?

Example: *The Parable of the Unjust Judge*
(Lk 18:1–5)
- Jesus is speaking to the disciples
- Jesus is talking about prayer
- The disciples compare to the widow
- Persevere in prayer!

An Allegory: Look for a second level of meaning by equating each element on the literal level with an element on the allegorical level.

Example: Widow—the disciples
Her requests—prayer
Judge—God

If this parable is interpreted as an allegory,
God appears to be an unjust judge

---

because she continued to ask, so too will the disciples benefit if they continue to pray. However, if, instead of drawing a single lesson from the parable based on a single comparison, we interpret the story as though it were an allegory, we get into trouble. If we interpret the story as an allegory, then each element of the literal level will stand for something on the intentional level. Therefore, if the story is about praying, and the widow stands for those who pray, then the unjust judge must stand for God. Since we know that Jesus was not teaching that God is an unjust judge, we see that interpreting the story as though it were an allegory leads to error.

In other words, we cannot claim that we are teaching what the Bible teaches if we allegorize a parable and draw a lesson from it that is different from the lesson which the Gospel editor intended to teach.

The Teaching

In order to understand what Matthew is teaching through the parable of the judgment of the nations we must respond to the four questions which we need to ask in order to discover the teaching of every parable. To whom is Jesus speaking? The disciples. What is the topic of conversation? The parable appears as one of many in Jesus' sermon about the end times. To whom in the story do the disciples compare? The disciples compare to those on the king's right and left who are being held accountable for their actions. What is Jesus teaching the disciples through the comparison? Jesus is teaching his disciples that they must care for the needy. The way they treat others, especially those in most need, is the way they are treating Christ himself. Jesus is teaching his disciples that in the "in between time," the time before the "second coming" or the "final judgment," the disciples are to feed the hungry and clothe the naked. They are to take care of those in need.

9. Matthew 22:1–14   Few are chosen (see also Lk 14:15–24)

The Misunderstanding

In both Matthew's and Luke's Gospels Jesus tells a parable about a master or king who holds a great banquet. When all is ready the invited guests do not come. In Matthew's account the king sends out his slaves a second time to gather the guests. The guests not only refuse to come, they kill the king's slaves. The king is so angry that he sends troops to

INTERPRETING PARABLES AND ALLEGORIES

A Parable: Look for one basic comparison between an element in the story and the audience listening to the story. The lesson comes from this comparison. Ask yourself:

- To whom is Jesus speaking?
- What's the topic?
- With what person or thing in the story does the audience compare?
- What lesson is drawn from this comparison?

Example: *The Parable of the Sower* (Mk 4:3–9)

- Jesus is speaking to the crowd
- Jesus is talking about being receptive
- The crowd compares to the soil
- Be good soil!

An Allegory: Look for a second level of meaning by equating each element on the literal level with an element on the allegorical level.

Example: Sower—God/a preacher/etc.
Seed— word of God
Those on edge of path—those from whom
    Satan takes the word
Patches of rock—those with no root
In thorns—those in whom the world chokes
    out the word so there is no fruit
Rich soil—those who accept the word and
    bear a rich harvest
Lesson—God's word can bear fruit only in a
    receptive person

If this parable is interpreted as an allegory the conclusion is still compatable with Scripture. In fact, an allegorical interpretation appears in Scripture (Mk 4:14–20).

destroy the murderers and burn their city. Again the king sends out his slaves to go and gather everyone they see, both good and bad. After the guests have gathered, the king comes into the banquet and sees a man there who is not wearing a wedding garment. The king says to the man, "'Friend, how did you get in here without a wedding robe?' And he was speechless. Then the king said to the attendants, 'Bind him hand and foot, and throw him into the outer darkness, where there will be weeping and gnashing of teeth.' For many are called, but few are chosen" (Mt 22:12–14). Many who read this parable conclude that God is prone to quick, unreasonable, and violent anger, that God's anger results in God's condemning people, and that very few people are actually going to make it to heaven. "Few are chosen." In fact, the parable does not support any of these conclusions.

Why the Error in Interpretation?

This parable lends itself to misinterpretation because it is so easily treated as though it were an allegory. Many elements in this story invite us to draw comparisons. However, if we allegorize this parable we fall into the same error that we fall into if we allegorize Luke's parable about the widow and the unjust judge. We say that the master or the king stands for God. This mistake in interpretation could cause us to attribute to God everything that is said about the king. Then we arrive at a number of false conclusions about God.

The Teaching

Again, in order to interpret this parable correctly, in order to understand what Matthew intended to teach by including this parable in his Gospel, we must identify the audience to whom Jesus is speaking, and ask what Jesus is teaching that specific audience. Remember, in a parable, as distinct from an allegory, the intended lesson is always drawn from this single comparison. In Matthew's Gospel, Jesus addresses the parable of the wedding banquet to the chief priests and Pharisees who had previously questioned his authority (see Mt 21:23–27). The chief priests and Pharisees compare to the variety of invited guests who fail

Contrasting the Two Literary Forms:

1. Comparisons— A parable is based primarily on a single comparison

   An allegory is based on many comparisons.

2. Audience— A parable is addressed specifically and personally to an audience. To understand the parable you must know the audience.

   An allegory is self-contained. You need not know the audience to understand it.

3. Forcefulness— A parable is a personal challenge to a new way of viewing reality and a new way of acting.

   An allegory may be an ingenious story which entertains, which teaches a moral about life generally or about "those other guys."

to respond to the invitation to the banquet. Some invited guests not only neglect to come to the banquet when all is ready, but they abuse and even kill the one who was sent to extend the invitation. Jesus is warning the chief priests and Pharisees that in rejecting him they are also rejecting an invitation to the kingdom of God. In Matthew's Gospel, Jesus' warning falls on deaf ears. The Pharisees' response is to try to figure out a way to trap Jesus (see Mt 22:15).

Why does the story include the detail about the invited guests killing the king's slaves and the king destroying their town? Scripture scholars suggest that Matthew has included this detail (it is not in Luke's account) because by the time Matthew is writing (80 A.D.) the Jewish leaders had in fact plotted Jesus' death, and Jerusalem had been destroyed (70 A.D.). Matthew is reminding his Jewish audience of these facts.

How are we to understand the words: "For many are called, but few are chosen"? Those "chosen" in the parable, in addition to having been called, are those who respond to the invitation. The man in the parable who is thrown out fails to be "chosen" because he is not properly dressed. His lack of proper dress symbolizes his lack of proper response. The Pharisees and scribes compare to this man. They are acting just as he is acting. Just as the man is completely unresponsive to the king's overtures, so are the Pharisees unresponsive to Jesus' overtures. The Pharisees, like the man, may feel that they have said "yes" to the invitation to the kingdom when, in fact, their lack of response to Jesus' teaching shows that they have not. The words, "Many are called but few are chosen," when addressed to the scribes and Pharisees, mean that few of the scribes and Pharisees are opening their hearts and minds to Jesus. Their lack of response will result in their excluding themselves from the kingdom.

10. Mark 3:38   The unforgivable sin (see also Mt 12:31)

The Misunderstanding

Is there such a thing as an unforgivable sin? Many people live under the burden of having done something so heinous in their own eyes that they think God could never actually forgive them. So they live in guilt and fear, believing that it is God's judgment of them rather than their judgment of themselves that is responsible for their ongoing misery. Do the words attributed to Jesus about an unforgivable sin support this frame of mind? Unfortunately, many misinterpret this passage and think the answer is "yes."

Why the Error in Interpretation?

It will probably come as no surprise to you that this error in interpretation comes from failing to put the passage in the context in which it appears in each Gospel. In both Mark and Matthew, Jesus is pictured as saying these words to his antagonists, the scribes (Mk 3:22) and

Pharisees (Mt 12:24), who consistently refuse to be open to Jesus, who refuse to accept the truth of what is happening right before their eyes. In each Gospel Jesus has "cast out devils," has cured demoniacs. In each Gospel the scribes and Pharisees have concluded that Jesus' power over evil forces must mean that Jesus is himself evil. "He has Beelzebub, and by the ruler of the demons he casts out demons" (Mk 3:22; Mt 12:24). In order to understand the intent of Jesus' words we must put them in the context of this charge.

The Teaching

The "unforgivable sin against the Holy Spirit" is the constant refusal to recognize good and so to name good "evil." This is an unforgivable sin not because God does not want to forgive but because the person who commits this sin remains incapable of acknowledging that he or she needs forgiveness and so never repents. Therefore, God's forgiveness, which is always offered, is never received. In both Mark and Matthew the scribes and Pharisees are witnessing Jesus' teachings and his mighty acts, and are attributing Jesus' power to Satan rather than to God. They insist that Jesus must be a sinner because he disobeys the law by healing on the sabbath. Jesus' power over evil spirits, therefore, must be because he is one of them. Jesus tries to reason with the scribes and Pharisees. He tells them that a house divided against itself will surely fall. He points out that they themselves have exorcists, and asks by whose power their own exorcists cast out devils. He confronts them with the one truth which they adamantly refuse to accept: "But if it is by the Spirit of God that I cast out demons, then the kingdom of God has come to you" (Mt 13:28). However, none of this helps. The scribes and Pharisees continue to reject Jesus, they continue to reject the Holy Spirit, and they continue to reject the kingdom of God. Their constant rejection leads to their lack of repentance. Their lack of repentance leads to their inability to accept forgiveness for their sins.

No passage in Scripture supports the idea that God refuses forgiveness to a repentant sinner. We will look at passages of Scripture that assure us of God's constant offer and desire to forgive in Chapter 4. For the time being, let it suffice to remember, "…there will be more joy in heaven over one sinner who repents than over ninety-nine righteous persons who need no repentance" (Lk 15:7).

11. Luke 17:10   Think of yourself as worthless

The Misunderstanding

In Luke's Gospel, Jesus tells his disciples to think of themselves as "worthless slaves." What could the intent of these words be? Does God want us to think little of ourselves, to assume a posture of servitude in relation to God and others? Some very "religious" people do have very little self-respect. Their lack of self-respect makes them vulnerable to mistreatment by others. They do not stand up for themselves because they do not believe that they deserve to be treated well. Is a "door mat" attitude a sign of true discipleship? Should a faithful disciple silently accept unjust treatment from others as an act of love for Christ? Many who love Christ are vulnerable to mistreatment by others because they misinterpret this passage and think that a true disciple should think of himself or herself as a "worthless slave."

Why the Error in Interpretation?

The word "slave" has a much more negative connotation for us than it would have had for Luke's audience. Slavery was simply part of the order of society in Jesus' world, and while Jesus taught that the way we treat every human being is the way we are treating the "Son of Man" (remember the parable of the judgment of the nations), Jesus did not explicitly attack the social order in which he lived, even though it included slaves. In many of the parables slaves appear as characters in the story, as we saw in the parable of the wedding feast. To be the slave of a king was a position of great honor. Mary refers to herself as a slave of the Lord, although we often translate her word as "handmaiden" (Lk 1:38, 48). The apostles refer to themselves as slaves of Christ (see Phil 1:1; Rom 1:1), and Jesus himself is referred to as a slave (see Phil 2:7). What is it about the image "slave" which made it an appropriate one to use so often? Why are the disciples advised to think of themselves as "worthless slaves"?

The Teaching

When Jesus teaches his disciples to think of themselves as "worthless slaves" he is warning them against the faults which he sees in the Pharisees. As religious leaders Jesus' disciples should not think of themselves as people who lord authority over others. Rather they should think of themselves as in service to others. Nor should they become filled with pride, thinking that by their good behavior they are becoming spiritually superior to others, that their "worth" is increasing in relation to others. Rather, they should realize that the opportunity to be a disciple and to be in service to others is not earned, but is a gift. So instead of being proud and self-righteous, seeking out positions of honor and wanting to be waited upon, as do the Pharisees, Jesus wants his disciples to be humble and grateful, seeking out those who lack positions of honor and finding ways to respond to their needs. So Jesus is not asking his disciples to think little of themselves or to adopt a subservient position. Nor is he asking them to think of themselves as "worthless." He is warning them against pride, against the idea that they are "earning" spiritual rewards, and so God is now in their spiritual debt.

Interestingly enough, the same image of "slave" is used with negative connotations to teach Christians that they, as well as every other person, are people of great dignity. Paul uses the image of slavery in a negative way when he tells the Romans, "For you did not receive a spirit of slavery to fall back into fear, but you have received a spirit of adoption. When we cry, 'Abba!' 'Father!' it is that very Spirit bearing witness with our spirit that we are children of God, and if children, then heirs, heirs of God and joint heirs with Christ..." (Rom 8:15–17). Jesus, too, is pictured as using the image of a slave or servant as a contrast to the high dignity of human beings when he says, "I do not call you servants any longer, because the servant does not know what the master is doing; but I have called you friends, because I have made known to you everything that I have heard from my Father" (Jn 15:15). We are friends of Christ, heirs of Christ. Each of us is a person of great dignity. No one of us has any reason to feel that we have earned our spiritual gifts, or that we are superior or inferior to any other person. We all have been chosen by God, and we all have equal dignity as children of God.

Images of God Which Scripture Does Not Support

In this chapter we have tried to understand why some of us have misunderstood Scripture and, consequently, have imagined God as unloving. We have tried to "undo" these negative images by explaining the mistakes in interpretation which lie behind the misunderstandings as well as the truths which the passages in question teach. We have shown that Scripture does not support a number of the ideas which people have about God.

1. God has not stayed mad and punished the whole human race for one couple's disobedience.
2. God does not turn people into pillars of salt if they "look behind."
3. God does not want us to hate and kill those whom we perceive as God's or our enemies.
4. God does not give Satan permission to reign over us for an assigned length of time.
5. God has not created a fiery pit in which God eternally tortures those who have sinned.
6. God does not want us to mistreat ourselves or others in the name of religion.
7. God particularly does not want us to neglect our families in the name of religion.
8. God does not eternally condemn nations and individuals for unconscious oversights.
9. God does not fail to invite some into the kingdom.
10. God does not refuse to forgive sins.
11. God does not want us to think of ourselves as worthless, or to accept the mistreatment of others as something which we deserve.

To the extent that any of these ideas have taken root in our minds and hearts, we have failed to understand, appreciate, or experience the fact that God is love. In Chapter 4 we will look at passages of Scripture which teach us very clearly the "good news" that God is love. But first we will look at the topic of prophecy, and in that context the book of Revelation. Misunderstandings about these two subjects have contributed to many people's misconceptions about God, and to their vulnerability when confronted by those who warn them about "doomsday" and about "the end of the world."

Chapter 3

Is the Book of Revelation Good News?

T he book of Revelation strikes fear into many people's hearts. This is true because many believe that the author of the book of Revelation foresaw specific, horrible events which will precede the end of the world. Since the world has not yet ended, many believe that the events "predicted" in the book of Revelation will happen in the future, or are happening right now.

This mistaken belief rests on two misunderstandings: one regarding the function of prophecy, the other regarding the literary form of the book of Revelation. In this chapter we will try to dispel both of these misunderstandings. First we will address the question, "Is the gift which God gave the prophets the ability to predict inevitable future events?" In order to answer this question, we will try to understand the crucial role which the prophets played in their own society, and the particular gift which God gave the prophets to enable them to fulfill their calling. Next we will look at passages from the prophetic books to see both what the selected passages originally meant, and what the early Church took the passages to mean in order to explain and teach what post-resurrection Christians had come to believe about Jesus Christ. We will discover that it is this use of the prophets' words by the early Church which has left many Christians with the mistaken impression that the prophets were fortune-tellers. With this knowledge about prophecy well in hand, we will look closely at the literary form of the book of Revelation in order to understand not only why the book does not say what many claim it says, but also what teaching the book does contain. We will discover that, like the Gospels, the book of Revelation is "good news."

What Is a Prophet?

In our culture we use the word "prophet" to refer to a person who predicts future events. If, in hindsight, we realize that the person was right we might call that person a true prophet. If the person turns out to be wrong we think of him or her as a false prophet. So in our culture a "fortune-teller" might be called a prophet because a fortune-teller also predicts future events. For us there is no clear distinction between the two.

In Old Testament times, on the other hand, seeking the advice of a fortune-teller was against the law, while listening to a prophet was a way of staying faithful to covenant love. There was a world of difference between the two. This distinction is made clear in the book of Deuteronomy when, as Moses promulgates the law, he says, "Let there not be found among you...a fortune-teller, soothsayer, charmer, diviner, or caster of spells, nor one who consults ghosts and spirits or seeks oracles from the dead. Anyone who does such things is an abomination to the Lord....Though these nations whom you are to dispossess listen to their soothsayers and fortune-tellers, the Lord, your God, will not permit you to do so. A prophet like me will the Lord, your God, raise up for you from among your own kinsmen; to him you shall listen" (Dt 18:10–12, 14–15).

This passage makes very clear that a prophet is not at all the same as a fortune-teller, or a person who claims to be able to prognosticate inevitable future events. To the extent that we see no distinction between them, we misunderstand the role of a prophet. Many Christians think that the prophets did prognosticate inevitable future events about Jesus. The reason we have this misunderstanding is that we never have asked ourselves what a prophet's contemporaries would have understood the prophet to be saying. Rather, we have read the words of the prophets only through the lens of Christ. We have heard passages from the prophets read in a worship setting, out of their Old Testament context, or we have read the words of the prophets quoted in the Gospels. This has left us with the impression that the spiritual gift of a prophet was precisely the ability to foresee future events in detail. In order to explain that prognostication was not the spiritual gift given to prophets, we first will have to define what spiritual gift the prophets did receive. Then we will look at the way believers used the words of the prophets when the age of the prophets ended. This will enable us to understand what the Gospel writers meant when they described details of Jesus' birth, public ministry, passion and death, and concluded by saying, "All this took place to fulfill what the Lord had said through the prophet…" (Mt 1:22).

The Spiritual Gift of a Prophet

The spiritual gift of a prophet was the ability to see the ramifications of present behavior in the light of covenant love. The word "prophet" means "one who speaks for another." In the context of the Bible, the "other" is God. So a biblical prophet is one who speaks for God. A prophet was able to see everything that was happening in his or her society in the context of covenant love. If people were sinning, the prophet recognized this behavior as incompatible with covenant love, and so warned the people that if they kept acting this way then disaster lay ahead. The prophet recognized what behavior was sinful, and realized that sinful behavior always leads to suffering. If the people were already suffering and were asking, "Where is God now?" the prophet would assure the people that God is always faithful to God's promises. So they could be sure that God was with them in their suffering and would send someone to save them. It was from this belief— that God could be trusted to send someone to save them—that the expectation of a "messiah" evolved. Since God is always faithful to covenant love, God would send a chosen person, an "anointed" (the word "messiah" means "anointed"), to defeat whoever was oppressing them.

So a prophet's words did pertain to the future, did warn or comfort people about the future. If the people were sinning the prophets warned of suffering, and if the people were suffering the prophets promised consolation. However, this is not the same thing at all as prognosticating inevitable events. A prophet was not saying that the suffering was inevitable, only that the suffering would occur if the people did not stop sinning. The prophet's words called for conversion. If the people's behavior changed, so would the ramifications of that behavior. So a "successful" prophet might be one who was heeded, and therefore helped people to avoid the catastrophes about which he warned them.

Jonah

One such "successful" prophet is humorously pictured in the story of Jonah, a story written to teach that God loves other nations. God tells Jonah to preach to the Ninevites, who had been Israel's worst enemy. Jonah did not want to preach to them because he did not consider them worth saving. But he did preach to them, and he was, to his own way of thinking, unfortunately successful in getting the Ninevites to reform, so that God did not destroy them. Jonah is disgusted with this turn of events. Since the Ninevites heeded his words, the destruction of which he warned would not occur. "But this was greatly displeasing to Jonah, and he became angry. 'I beseech you, Lord,' he prayed, 'is not this what I said while I was still in my own country? This is why I fled at first to Tarshish. I knew that you are a gracious and merciful God, slow to anger, rich in clemency, loathe to punish. And now, Lord, please take my life from me; for it is better for me to die than to live'" (Jon 4:1–3). Jonah is a parody of a true prophet. Jonah blames, rather than praises, God for being loving. He prefers to see the destruction occur rather than have the Ninevites repent and be saved. (For a fuller treatment of the story see chapter 4, pp. 124-27.)

The spiritual gift of the prophet, then, was the spiritual perception to understand covenant love and to be able to correctly assess the ramifications of present behavior in the light of covenant love. The prophet functioned as God's voice; the prophet spoke for God.

The Age of the Prophets

The age of the prophets and the age of the kings are, for the most part, the same. Prophecy was born with kingship. Scripture scholars think that when the word "prophet" is applied to Moses, we are reading a hindsight application. In other words, neither Moses nor his contemporaries would have referred to Moses as a "prophet." Later, however, after the role of the prophet was firmly established, when the stories of Moses were told, Moses was called a "prophet" because he functioned as a prophet: Moses spoke for God.

After the time of Moses and the Exodus (1250 B.C.) the people finally made it to the Holy Land, to Canaan. However, during this

PROPHETS

Definition of a Prophet: One who speaks for God
Role of a Prophet: To call Israel to fidelity to covenant love

1. Monotheism
2. Morality
3. Messianism

Kings & Events

1020–1000 B.C. Saul	Samuel	1020 B.C.
1000–961 B.C. David	Nathan	1000 B.C.
922 B.C. Division of the Kingdom (Judah [S] Israel [N])		
869–850 B.C. Ahab	Elijah (N)	850 B.C.
786–746 B.C. Jeroboam II	Amos (N)	750 B.C.
	Hosea (N)	745 B.C.
735–715 B.C. Ahaz	I Isaiah (S)	742–700 B.C.
	Micah (S)	722–701 B.C.
721 B.C. Fall of Samaria		
715–687 B.C. Hezekiah		
640–609 B.C. Josiah	Zephaniah (S)	628–622 B.C.
	Jeremiah (S)	626–587 B.C.
	Nahum (S)	612 B.C.
609–598 B.C. Jehoiakim		
	Habakkuk (S)	605 B.C.
597–587 B.C. Zedekiah		
	Ezekiel (S)	593–573 B.C.
587–537 B.C. Babylonian Exile	Obadiah (S)	After 587 B.C.
	II Isaiah (S)	After 540 B.C.
537 B.C. Persian Rule	III Isaiah (S)	After 537 B.C.
	Haggai	520–515 B.C.
	Zechariah	520–515 B.C.
	Joel	500–350 B.C.
	Malachi	500–450 B.C.

period of their history they did not have a king. The people were organized into "tribes," and there was no single leader over all the tribes. During the two hundred years that they slowly conquered those who were already living in Canaan, they acted as a unified whole only when they needed to band together to face a common enemy. Those who rose to leadership during this period were called "judges," and so this period of their history (roughly 1200 B.C.–1000 B.C.) was called the period of the judges.

When the Philistines became powerful, they fought the Israelites and captured the ark of the covenant, the box which contained the law, the symbol of God's presence with God's people. This was a catastrophe. Some of the people believed that they should have "a king like other nations." With a king they would be better able to ward off their political enemies. Others believed that if Israel had a king like other nations, the people would forget who the king really is: Yahweh. Eventually, Israel did get a king like other nations, first Saul and then David, but Israel also got prophets who would remind the king that he himself was not God.

Nathan and David

The wisdom of having someone who speaks for God, even to the king, is evident when we look at the events that occurred under the greatest of all kings, King David. David united the twelve tribes, defeated the Philistines, and brought the ark of the covenant to Jerusalem. David also saw Uriah's wife, Bathsheba, bathing, and wanted her. So he had her brought to the palace; he slept with her, and she became pregnant. In order to hide his sin, David tried to make it appear that Uriah had fathered the child. When this became impossible, David arranged for Uriah's death. So the greatest of all kings was guilty of adultery and murder. It seemed that David had forgotten that God, not he, was really king. David needed someone to remind him of this fact.

Nathan was the prophet during David's reign. It was his role to speak for God to the nation. So Nathan had to call David to repentance. We read the account of what Nathan said to David when "Yahweh sent Nathan the prophet to David" in 2 Samuel 12:1–15. Nathan tells David a parable. This parable functions just as we described parables as functioning in Chapter 2. The story is about a rich man who owns many flocks and a poor man who owns a ewe lamb, which he loves. When a traveler comes, the rich man insists that the poor man's single ewe lamb be killed and prepared for the guest. David does not realize that this story is about him, so he passes judgment on the characters in the story. David considers the behavior of the rich man terribly reprehensible, and so he says, "As the Lord lives, the man who has done this merits death!" (2 Sm 12:5). David compares to the rich man. Just as the rich man took the poor man's lamb, so David took Uriah's wife. Nathan brings home his message by saying to David, "You are the man!" (2 Sm 12:7). Nathan points out to David that the ramification of sin is suffering.

As long as Israel had kings, Israel had prophets. The age of Israel's kings ended after the Babylonian Exile (587 B.C.–537 B.C.). The Babylonian Exile was the second most traumatic time in the whole history of the nation. Ever since the time of Nathan and David, the people had taken the existence of the kingdom, the king in David's line, and the temple which had been built in Jerusalem as the outward signs of covenant love (see 2 Sm 7:1–17). They believed that none of these could ever be destroyed. Much to their horror, the Babylonians conquered them, destroyed the temple, murdered the king's sons, and physically moved much of the population to Babylon. This forced the people to ask, "Is God still our God? Are we still God's people?" During the exile, and immediately after the exile, the Jews still had prophets. However, after they returned from exile they did not have their own nation, nor their own king. Therefore, soon after their return, the age of the prophets ended. We hear the pain of this loss expressed in Psalm 74: "They said in their hearts, 'Let us destroy them; burn all the shrines of God in the land.' Deeds on our behalf we do not see; there is no prophet now, and no one of us knows how long…" (Ps 74:8–9).

The Words of the Prophets Are "Fulfilled"

With the end of the age of the prophets, people wondered where they were to turn to hear God's voice. The function of the prophets was carried on not by prophets, but by scribes. The scribes did not have the same spiritual gift which God had given the prophets. They did not "speak for God." When they spoke they did not say, "Yahweh says this...." They did not attribute God's authority to their own words. Rather, they continued to attribute God's authority to the words of the law (i.e. the first five books of the Old Testament) and the words of the past prophets. They examined these words in the context of their own lives, and tried to find God's hidden purposes for them expressed in the words of the law and the prophets. In other words, they often *reinterpreted* the original meaning of the words to make the words applicable to their own setting. Based on their belief that God's will and God's way could be discerned by reinterpreting the words of the law and the prophets, the scribes scoured these words to help their contemporaries make right choices, and to help them interpret the meaning of contemporary events. This practice of the time was an act of faith in God's providence and in God's purposes in history.

The reinterpretation of the words of the prophets which resulted from this act of faith generally took three forms: these can be described as "typology," as "allegory," and as "prophecy and fulfillment." Evidence that the scribes commonly practiced these three ways of reinterpreting the words of the law and the prophets is present in the New Testament. We can illustrate them by looking at some of Paul's letters. Paul had been well educated in the traditions of the Jews, and wrote utilizing the beliefs and customs of the time.

Typology

"Typology" is a word which traditionally has been used to refer to the fact that Old Testament people and events, in addition to their own historic role in revealing God's will for God's people, can be seen as "types," or as "foreshadowing" for New Testament people and events. To illustrate this we need only turn to Paul's first letter to the Corinthians. Paul says, "I do not want you to be unaware, brothers, that our ancestors were all under the cloud and all passed through the sea, and all of them were baptized into Moses in the cloud and in the sea. All ate the same spiritual food, and all drank the same spiritual drink, for they drank from a spiritual rock that followed them, and the rock was the Christ. Yet God was not pleased with most of them, for they were struck down in the desert. These things happened as examples for us, so that we might not desire evil things, as they did…" (1 Cor 10:1–6).

Here Paul is drawing an analogy between the account of the exodus and the journey of each Christian, but he is doing more than merely drawing a comparison. He is seeing the journey of the exodus as a "type" or "foreshadowing" of the journey of Christians. He is seeing the rock from which the Israelites found water as a "type" or "foreshadowing" of Christ. He is seeing the sins of the ancestors as a "type" or "foreshadowing" of the sins of Christians. He is warning the Corinthians to learn from this example so that they do not make the same mistakes as did their ancestors in faith. In other words, the time in the desert and the water from the rock are seen both as historical events and as "types" of later events. God mysteriously revealed God's will through the original events so that they functioned as revelatory "types" or "foreshadowings" of events which were to follow. By scouring the words of the law and the prophets, those who lived later could make sense out of their own experience, and discern God's will for them in the context of their own lives, by recognizing an additional layer of meaning in the original words.

Allegory

Paul also makes use of allegory. You may remember that we defined allegory in Chapter 2. In an allegory there are two levels of meaning, the literal level and the intentional level. Each element of the literal story stands for something on the intentional level. Paul makes use of allegory in his letter to the Galatians when he says: "Tell me, you who want to be under the law, do you not listen to the law? For it is written that Abraham had two sons, one by the slave woman and the other by the freeborn woman. The son of the slave woman was born naturally, the son of the freeborn through a promise. Now this is an allegory. These women represent two covenants. One was from Mount Sinai, bearing children for slavery; this is Hagar. Hagar represents Sinai, a mountain in Arabia; it corresponds to the present Jerusalem, for she is in slavery along with her children. But the Jerusalem above is freeborn, and she is our mother.…Now you, brothers, like Isaac, are children of the promise. But just as then the child of the flesh persecuted the child of the spirit, it is the same now….Therefore, brothers, we are children not of the slave woman but of the freeborn woman" (Gal 4:21–26, 28–29, 31).

In this passage Paul is taking a story in the law about historical people, the story of Abraham, Sarah, and the slave Hagar in the book of Genesis, and he is interpreting the story as an allegory. He is saying that Judaizers, who want the Galatians to believe that in order to be Christians they must follow the Jewish law, compare to Ishmael, who is the child of the slave, Hagar. On the other hand, the Galatians, who are free of the law, compare to Isaac, who is the child of Sarah, the child of the promise. Through his allegorical interpretation Paul is teaching the Galatians that they must not become slaves of the Jewish law. They have been saved, not by obedience to the law, but by Christ's passion, death, and resurrection. They are children of the promise, not of the law, and they should not let the Judaizers persuade them to become slaves to the law.

Paul does not arrive at his conclusions by reading the law. He arrives at his conclusions by reflecting on the meaning of his lived experience, under the inspiration of the Holy Spirit. However, in teaching these conclusions to his contemporaries, he utilizes the customs of the time. He looks for words in the law or in the prophets that, if reinterpreted, could be used to illustrate his point. By arguing from Scripture, Paul is expressing his faith that he has correctly discerned what have been God's hidden purposes all along. Paul was recognized by the early Church as having been inspired, and so Paul's letters became part of the canon. Christians accept Paul's teaching as true.

Promise and Fulfillment

The third way in which the Jews after the Babylonian exile, and the early Christians, used the words of the law and the prophets to teach their contemporaries is "prophecy and fulfillment." This is the use which we see in the Gospels when we read the phrase, "This took place to fulfill what the Lord had said through the prophet…" (Mt 1:22). Notice, this is "prophecy and fulfillment," not, "prognostication and fulfillment." In order to assure that you do not hear the phrase "prophecy and fulfillment" as "prognostication and fulfillment," I will refer to this method as "promise and fulfillment." The words of the prophets were speaking of the future, not in the sense of prognostication, but in the sense of reminding their contemporaries that God would be faithful to God's promises. God's fidelity is part of covenant love. So we could understand the phrase to mean, "All this took place to fulfill God's promise, a promise which the prophets understood and about which they taught." It is this Jewish custom, employed in the Gospels, that has resulted in so many Christians misunderstanding the nature of prophecy. To illustrate this use of the words of the law and the prophets, we will turn to an example from the Gospel.

In Matthew's Gospel we read that an angel appeared to Joseph and explained to him that Mary would conceive through the power of the Holy Spirit, and that the child was to be named Jesus because he would save his people from their sins. Then Matthew adds, "All this took place to fulfill what the Lord had said through the prophet: 'Behold, the virgin shall be with child and bear a son, and they shall name him "Emmanuel," which means "God is with us" ' "(Mt 1:22–23).

Many Christians have understood this passage to mean that the prophet who is quoted, Isaiah, foresaw the fact that Mary would conceive a child without having had sexual intercourse, and that God would become a human being. In fact, neither of these events was foreseen or expected. To understand what the prophet was saying, and how Matthew used the words to teach the significance of the events that had occurred in and through Jesus Christ, we must put the prophet's words in the context in which they originally appear.

Isaiah and Ahaz

The passage in question appears in Isaiah 7:14: "...the virgin shall be with child, and bear a son, and shall name him Immanuel." These words are spoken by the prophet Isaiah to King Ahaz (735 B.C.–715 B.C.). What would King Ahaz and his contemporaries have understood by the words? To answer this question we will need to refer to several more verses from Isaiah, verses which precede and follow the passage in question. Isaiah begins by telling us the political context for the conversation that will follow. Two kings are threatening to attack Jerusalem, the king of Aram and the king of the northern king-dom, Israel. These two small nations are threatening to attack because they themselves are being threatened by the Assyrians. They want King Ahaz, the king of the southern kingdom, to join with them against the Assyrians. Ahaz feels more threatened by these two nations than he does by the Assyrians. "When word came to the house of David that Aram was encamped in Ephraim, the heart of the king and the heart of the people trembled, as the trees of the forest tremble in the wind" (Is 7:2).

God sends the prophet Isaiah to Ahaz to remind him of covenant love. God has promised to protect the house of David. Ahaz should not put his trust in an alliance with these two small nations, in the "Syro-Ephramite alliance," nor in the Assyrians. Rather, Ahaz should put his trust in Yahweh. Isaiah is reminding Ahaz of God's fidelity to the house of David when he says that God will give him a sign. "Therefore the Lord himself will give you this sign: the virgin shall be with child, and bear a son, and shall name him Immanuel. He shall be living on curds and honey by the time he learns to reject the bad and choose the good. For before the child learns to reject the bad and choose the good, the land of those two kings whom you dread shall be deserted" (Is 7:14–16).

Isaiah is telling Ahaz that the line of David is continuing, that he and his wife, a young maiden, will soon have a son, and that this son will not be very old before the two nations which are threatening Judah will themselves be defeated. They are only a temporary threat. The words do not say that the virgin will conceive without having had intercourse. No one expected such an event to occur. The Hebrew word translated "virgin" could just as well have been translated "maiden." The Hebrew word draws no distinction between a maiden and a virgin. It was when the Hebrew was translated into Greek, in the Septuagint, that the nar-rower meaning of the word "virgin" was introduced. Nor do the words say that God will become a human being, only that God will be with Ahaz's descendants, just as God had been with David, with Solomon, and with all the kings of the house of David.

As things worked out, Ahaz did not heed Isaiah's words. Instead of trusting Yahweh, Ahaz decided to trust the Assyrians. "...Ahaz sent messengers to Tiglath-pileser, king of Assyria, with the plea: 'I am your servant and your son. Come up and rescue me from the clutches of the king of Aram and the king of Israel, who are attacking me.' Ahaz took the silver and gold that were in the temple of the Lord and in the palace treasuries and sent them as a present to the king of Assyria, who listened to him and moved against Damascus, which he captured" (2 Kgs 17:7–9).

Even though Ahaz was not faithful to God, God was faithful to the house of David. Ahaz did have a son, Hezekiah, who turned out to be a more faithful king than was Ahaz. The author of 2 Kings, in describing Hezekiah, says, "He pleased the Lord, just as his forefather David had done…. He put his trust in the Lord, the God of Israel; and neither before him nor after him was there anyone like him among all the kings of Judah. Loyal to the Lord, Hezekiah never turned away from him, but observed the commandments which the Lord had given to Moses. The Lord was with him, and he prospered in all that he set out to do" (2 Kgs 18:3, 5–7). The Lord was with Hezekiah, just as the prophet Isaiah had said. The prophet had understood covenant love, and had known that God would be faithful to God's promises.

Post-Resurrection Interpretations

Isaiah's words did not lead anyone to expect that a woman would conceive a child by the power of the Holy Spirit. Nor did Isaiah's words lead anyone to expect that God would become a human being. Jesus' disciples did not expect these events to occur, nor, during the time of the historical Jesus, would they have been able to claim that such events had occurred. The disciples realized what had occurred only in the light of the resurrection. In order to understand and explain the events that occurred in their midst, the disciples turned to the words of the law and the prophets. Here they found that God had already given them the concepts and the vocabulary to explain what, in the light of the resurrection, they believed had occurred.

The New Testament constantly illustrates this process in the way in which it quotes the Old Testament. In fact, Luke's Gospel pictures the risen Christ himself turning to the words of the law and the prophets to explain God's hidden purposes as they had been fulfilled in him. Shortly after the crucifixion, two disciples are on the road to Emmaus. Their hopes are dashed. They had expected Jesus to be the messiah, to

THE PROCESS WHICH MAKES IT APPEAR TO CHRISTIANS THAT PROPHETS ARE FORTUNE-TELLERS

1. Events take place (David was a great king; the king-dom was divided; enemies threatened).

2. The prophets speak with insight about present events ("woe" if people are sinning; "weal" if people are in distress).

3. People form expectations based on past and present experiences and hope (e.g. things are bad now, but God will save us through someone like David).

4. More events take place. (Jesus is conceived by Mary through the Holy Spirit. After his resurrection his followers experience his presence and come to realize that God became a human being.)

5. The prophets' words are reinterpreted, "fulfilled," in the light of these new events. The words take on a second level of meaning. There is not a claim that the original speaker (the prophet) intended to say what the words, in hindsight, have been taken to mean.

6. Response: wonder at God's mysterious ways; awe; praise; thanksgiving.

establish a power base from which he could free them from the Romans. Instead, Jesus had received a death sentence at the hands of the Romans. As they are walking along, the risen Christ is pictured as joining them. They do not recognize Jesus. Jesus asks them what they were discussing. They tell him how disappointed they are. "We were hoping that he would be the one to redeem Israel..." (Lk 24:21). Jesus says to them " 'Oh, how foolish you are! How slow of heart to believe all that the prophets spoke! Was it not necessary that the Messiah should suffer these things and enter into his glory?' Then, beginning with Moses and all the prophets, he interpreted to them what referred to him in all the scriptures" (Lk 24:25–27).

A Suffering Servant

One reason why the disciples had such a difficult time realizing who Jesus was is that they did not expect the messiah to suffer and die. In fact, their idea of a messiah precluded the possibility that the messiah would suffer and die. Their image of the messiah, based on the words of the prophets, was that the messiah would be a great political leader who would conquer their political enemies and return control of the Holy Land to them. This idea was completely incompatible with what actually occurred.

However, after Jesus died and rose from the dead, his Jewish followers, as was their custom, turned to the words of the prophets to find the words and images which would enable them to comprehend and explain what had taken place. They turned to the words of Second Isaiah's "suffering servant songs" (see Is 42:1–7; 49:1–9; 50:4–9; 52:13–53:12). In these passages a prophet, now called Second Isaiah, who lived during the Babylonian Exile, was helping his fellow Israelites make some sense out of their suffering and loss. Second Isaiah thought of the nation in exile as God's "suffering servant." He taught that God was accomplishing something wonderful and new through God's people, even while they were in exile in Babylon. Second Isaiah knew that God was still being faithful. He taught that God would use the Israelites' suffering as a light to other nations. Other nations would come to a knowledge of Yahweh through them. Second Isaiah says: "If he (i.e. the nation) gives his life as an offering for sin, he shall see his descendants in a long life, and the will of the Lord shall be accomplished through him. Because of his affliction he shall see the light in fullness of days; through his suffering, my servant shall justify many, and their guilt he shall bear. Therefore I will give him his portion among the great...because he surrendered himself to death and was counted among the wicked; and he shall take away the sins of many, and win pardon for their offenses" (Is 53:10b–12).

These suffering servant songs were not thought of as messianic prophecies until after Jesus suffered, died, and rose from the dead. In hindsight, in the light of these events, the early Christians reread the suffering servant songs and found in them a meaning which no one saw before. Something completely unexpected, and not understood at the time it occurred, was later described as having been "announced beforehand through the mouth of the prophets." In Peter's early preaching he is pictured as saying to those who crucified Jesus, "Now I know, brothers, that you acted out of ignorance, just as your leaders did; but God has thus brought to fulfillment what he had announced beforehand through the mouth of all the prophets, that his messiah would suffer" (Acts 3:17–18).

The claim is not that the prophets knowingly announced these things, but that God announced them through the words of the prophets. God was mysteriously at work, through events and through the words of the prophets, preparing and forming God's people to be

---

MESSIANIC PROPHECIES

l. Some Great and Glorious King Prophecies
2 Sam 7:1–17
Ps 132:11–18
Is 7:10–14
Is 11:1–9
Mi 5:1
Ez 34:23–31
Dan 7:9–14

II. Some Suffering Servant Prophecies
Is 42:1–7
Is 49:1–9
Is 50:4–9
Is 52:13-53:12

III. The Two Concepts Are Joined in Christ
Mk 8:27–33
Mk 9:30–32
Mk 10:32–34

able to conceptualize and speak about the profound and unimagined events which would occur in their midst.

"Typology," "allegory," and the "promise-fulfillment" motif were methods of interpretation which enabled generations of people to probe and to explain to others the meaning of the events in their own lives in the context of their inherited religious traditions, in the context of God's love for God's people. In the process of trying to understand God's purposes in events, hidden meanings of scripture were discovered.

The Devil Can Quote Scripture

However, what is true in our day was true in Jesus' time: The fact that a person quotes Scripture to support his or her point of view does not guarantee that the point of view is correct. Both those who correctly understood and those who misunderstood could use Scripture to probe the meaning of events. We see this when Jesus is arguing with his antagonists. Both Jesus and those with whom he disagrees quote Scripture. In fact, during Jesus' temptation in the wilderness, even the devil is pictured as quoting both Deuteronomy and the Psalms (see Mt 4:1–11).

A good example of how Scripture is quoted in arguments occurs in the conversation between Jesus and the Pharisees over whether or not divorce is allowed. Both Jesus and the Pharisees turn to the law to support their point of view (see Mk 10:1–12). The Pharisees quote Moses and say, "Moses permitted him to write a bill of divorce and dismiss her" (Mk 10:4). Even though the Pharisees have quoted the law, Jesus does not accept their conclusion. Jesus too turns to Scripture and reinterprets a passage from the law to support his teaching. "But from the beginning of creation, 'God made them male and female. For this reason a man shall leave his father and mother and be joined to his wife, and the two shall become one flesh.' So they are no longer two but one flesh. Therefore what God has joined together, no human being must separate" (Mk 10:6–9). Jesus uses a passage from Genesis 2:24, a passage which is not, in its original context, answering the question which the Pharisees have asked, to support his teaching that divorce is not allowed.

Just as those who correctly understood the meaning of Jesus' suffering and death turned to Scripture to support their point of view, so did those who failed to recognize Jesus as the messiah. The law had placed a curse on anyone who dies hanging on a tree. "If a man guilty of a capital offense is put to death and his corpse hung on a tree, it shall not remain on the tree overnight. You shall bury it the same day; otherwise, since God's curse rests on him who hangs on a tree, you will defile the land which the Lord, your God is giving you as an inheritance" (Dt 21:22–23). Jesus' death fit this description (see Gal 3:13). So those who did not believe that Jesus was the messiah could quote this passage to support their belief. It is because of this passage in the law that Jesus' death on a cross is referred to as a "shame" (see Heb 12:2).

A Custom of the Time

Thus we see that quoting Scripture to support a point of view is a custom which began well before Jesus' life on earth. Jesus, who grew up with this practice, himself turned to Scripture to reinforce his teaching. Jesus' followers, too, turned to Scripture to find the concepts and the vocabulary to explain what they had come to know through experience. Those who were not followers of Jesus used the same method to argue their point, both during Jesus' lifetime and after Jesus' death. As is true today, the fact that a person quotes Scripture to support what he or she is teaching does not necessarily mean that what the person is teaching is right or wrong. Both those who understand the truth and those who do not can quote passages of Scripture out of context to support what they are saying. It is not wrong to do this. However, it can lead to error if the speaker or the listener believes that the fact of quoting Scripture proves the truth of the statement.

We have now reviewed the function of a prophet. We have distinguished the prophet's function from that of a fortune-teller. We have explained that the prophet's words were not prognosticating inevitable future events, but were teaching the prophet's contemporaries the ramifications of covenant love. We have examined the ways in which the scribes turned to the words of the law and the prophets to seek direction and to uncover God's hidden purposes in the events of their own generation. We have seen that in using the prophets' words to explain the meaning of subsequent events, the words were discovered to have a level of meaning which was not part of the intent of the original prophet. God had provided the words and concepts necessary to conceptualize and explain the meaning of what had occurred in and through Jesus Christ. We have come to understand that the phrase, "to fulfill the words of the prophet," refers to this habit of reinterpreting the words to explain the significance of subsequent events.

Jesus: The Fulfillment of the Law and the Prophets

You may remember that, in Matthew's Gospel, Jesus is pictured as saying, "Do not think that I have come to abolish the law or the prophets. I have come not to abolish but to fulfill" (Mt 5:17). You may also remember that one of the remarks which the crowd makes about Jesus is that "he taught them as one having authority, and not as their scribes" (Mt 7:28). Jesus did teach with more authority than did the scribes or the prophets. As we have seen, the scribes did not use their own words to teach, but turned to a reinterpretation of the words of the law and the prophets. The prophets, who spoke for God, attributed their words to God by speaking in the form of an oracle: "Yahweh says this…." Jesus, however, did not merely quote the law and the prophets, he "fulfilled" them. Jesus said, "You have heard that it was said to your ancestors…" and Jesus would quote the law. But then Jesus would go on to say, "But I say to you…" and Jesus would give a teaching of his own that was much more demanding than was the law (see Mt 5:21–46). Jesus taught with his own authority, an authority given him by the Father. The law and the prophets were great revelations of God's love for God's people. However, Jesus was the fulfillment of the revelation of God's love. In Jesus all was made new, including the meaning of the words of the law and the prophets.

The Book of Revelation

Now that we understand the function of prophecy we will better be able to correctly understand the book of Revelation. As we have already said, most of the misinterpretations of the book of Revelation are based on two misunderstandings: a misunderstanding about the function of prophecy and a misunderstanding about the literary form of the book. So to begin our discussion we will compare the book of Revelation to prophecy, and apply what we have already learned about the function of prophecy to this work.

The Book of Revelation Compared to Prophecy

Just as prophecy is not fortune-telling, so the book of Revelation is not fortune-telling. The book of Revelation is not prognosticating inevitable future events which will precede the "end of the world." The truth of these statements will become clear as we compare the book of Revelation to prophecy, and as we explain the literary form of the book, a form called "apocalyptic" literature.

Nevertheless, we are all familiar with some people's attempts to apply the symbolic language in the book of Revelation to institutions and people of our own time. Not too long ago, when I was giving a talk in a Roman Catholic church, I came out to find a tract under my windshield wiper that claimed that the Roman Catholic Church is "the whore of Babylon" and that the Pope is "666." No matter what institution or person is the object of such an interpretation, the person offering the interpretation is simply revealing his or her own hate and prejudice. The interpretation has absolutely nothing to do with the purpose or meaning of the book of Revelation.

The book of Revelation is similar to prophecy because it has the same function as prophecy. Remember, prophecy had two functions: to warn of inevitable suffering if people continued to sin, and to promise "salvation" if people were suffering. The book of Revelation was written to fulfill the second function. In fact, all apocalyptic literature is written to fulfill this second function. Apocalyptic literature is written to people who are suffering persecution. It is reminding them that God is always faithful to God's promises, so God can be depended upon to save them. Everyone should "keep the faith!" In other words, the book of Revelation is calling people to be faithful to covenant love, and is assuring those in the audience that God will be faithful to them.

Not only does the book of Revelation fulfill the function of prophecy, the book refers to itself as "prophecy." At the beginning of the book we read, "Blessed is the one who reads aloud the words of the prophecy" (Rv 1:1), and at the end, "Blessed is the one who keeps the words of the prophecy of this book" (Rv 22:7). This means, "Blessed are those who are faithful to covenant love, even at times of terrible persecution."

Since the book functions as prophecy, the narrator (i.e. the voice telling the story) is commissioned as a prophet. "You must again prophesy about many peoples and nations and tongues and kings" (Rv 10:11). The narrator does just that. However, the narrator does not use the traditional literary form which prophets use, the "oracle." Rather, the narrator uses two other forms simultaneously, "apocalyptic literature," and "letter."

Conventions of the Forms

Since the form "letter" is one with which we are familiar in our own culture, we will use this form to explain a concept which we will need in order to be able to understand the book of Revelation. This is the concept of "literary conventions." Different literary forms employ different "conventions." For instance, the form "letter" includes an inside address, a salutation, the body of the letter, a farewell, and a signature which reveals the identity of the sender. It is a convention in letter writing to address the person to whom we are writing as "Dear." Usually, "dear" is a way of addressing a person who actually is "dear" to us. But, when we write a letter, we address a complete stranger as "dear," even a group of strangers. We might begin a business letter to people whom we have never met with the words, "Dear Colleagues."

In other words, because the use of the word "dear" in the salutation is a convention of the form "letter," the convention "overrides" the meaning of the word. If I were to write a "Dear John" letter, the fact that I begin with the word "Dear" does not constitute misleading John. I am not expressing my affection. I'm just beginning a letter.

If one misunderstands the conventions of a form one could be misled. I saw an instance of this in the letters to the editor of a newspaper. A person wrote the editor to discuss a religious subject and closed his letter "Fr. John Doe." The next week someone who knew the author of the letter, and knew that he was not a priest, wrote and accused him of claiming to be a priest, and therefore claiming knowledge and authority which he did not have. The next week a letter appeared explaining

BOOK OF REVELATION
COMPARED TO PROPHECY

1. The book is referred to as "prophecy." "Blessed is the one who reads aloud the words of the prophecy" (Rv 1:1).

   "Blessed is the one who keeps the words of the prophecy of this book"(Rv 22:7).

2. The narrator is commissioned as a prophet. "You must again prophesy about many peoples and nations and tongues and kings" (Rv 10:11).

3. The book of Revelation has the same function as prophecy. It calls people to fidelity in covenant relationship."Persevere and have hope. God will save."

THE FORM OF EACH OF THE "LETTERS"
TO THE SEVEN CHURCHES COMPARED
TO PROPHETIC WRITING

- Each begins with a commissioning, with Christ telling John to write

- An "I know" section which functions as a prophetic oracle:
  - Praise
  - Correction
  - Call to repentence
  - Warning of ramifications of actions: punishment or salvation

- Conclusion: A promise of salvation and a command to listen

that the original letter writer had not meant to claim to be a priest. In his country, one ends a letter with "Fr." meaning "from," to say whom the letter is from. The "Fr." was replacing our farewell, not claiming priesthood. To misunderstand the conventions of a form can lead to a misunderstanding of the intention of the author. In Scripture, as we said before, to misunderstand the intention of an author is to misunderstand the revelation.

The author of the book of Revelation observes the conventions of letter writing not in the form of each of his seven letters, but rather at the beginning and end of his book. Before describing the vision of Christ with which the book begins, John says, "To the seven churches in the province of Asia: John wishes you grace and peace—from him who is and who was and who is to come..." (Rv 1:4). This is the conventional way to begin a letter. First the recipient of the letter is named, then the sender, followed by a greeting and a doxology. The conventional ending for a letter, a benediction, appears at the conclusion of the book: "The grace of the Lord Jesus be with you all. Amen" (Rv 22:21).

The Conventions of Apocalyptic Literature

More important to our understanding of the book of Revelation than the form and conventions of a "letter," however, is our understanding of the form and conventions of "apocalyptic literature."

As we have already said, the function of apocalyptic literature is to offer hope to those facing persecution. Many of the conventions of this kind of writing are the result of its function. Because the intended audience is in mortal danger, apocalyptic literature is written in a kind of code that only the intended audience would be able to understand. Those doing the persecuting would not be able to understand this code. Because the message is to trust God's promises and God's love, even in the worst of circumstances, conventions are used which serve to teach that God is in control of the course of history. No person or evil is more powerful than God and God's love. No power on earth can thwart God's ultimate purposes.

Apocalyptic literature was a very popular form of literature for a four hundred year period, two hundred years before Jesus and two hundred years after. The conventions were entirely recognizable to the intended audience. They would not have misled a contemporary audience any more than the word "dear" at the beginning of a letter would mislead us. However, the conventions have misled many in our own generation simply because apocalyptic literature is not part of our culture.

These are the conventions of apocalyptic literature:

1. The work claims to contain a hidden revelation which was known only to God.
2. The narrator claims that God or an angel gave the revelation to him.
3. The narrator claims to have received the revelation in a vision.
4. The revelation is said to be in a sealed book which is to be opened only at the "end time."
5. The revelation is communicated through symbolic language and numbers.
6. Usually, although not in the book of Revelation, the book is attributed to a venerated figure of a past generation.
7. Usually, although not in the book of Revelation, the setting of the book is a past time, so past historic events are presented as though they will be future events.

The book of Daniel, the other example of an apocalyptic book which we have in Scripture, observes all of these conventions, even the last two. The book of Revelation does not observe all of the conventions. Nevertheless, as we shall see, it does "acknowledge" them.

Apocalyptic Literature Not Prognostication

Let us begin our discussion of these conventions, and of the misunderstandings which have resulted from not realizing that they are conventions, with the last two. It is a convention in apocalyptic literature for the writer to attribute his work to a venerable person from the past. This person receives the vision and is told to put it in a sealed book. The book is to be opened only at the end time. Since the sealed book is the one actually being read by the audience, this means that the "end time" is the time of the first generation to read the book. If the author were not trying to tell them that they are living at the "end time," then they would not be reading the book at all since the book was to remain sealed until the end time.

CONVENTIONS OF APOCALYPTIC LITERATURE

1. The work contains a hidden revelation which was known only to God.

2. God or an angel gave the revelation to a person.

3. The person receives the revelation in a vision.

4. The revelation is in a sealed book.

5. The revelation is to be opened only at the end of time.

6. The revelation is communicated through symbolic language and numbers.

7. The book is attributed to a venerated figure of a past generation.

8. The setting of the book is a past time, so past historic events are presented as though they will be future events.

WAYS IN WHICH THE BOOK OF REVELATION DEPARTS FROM THE CONVENTIONS

1. The work is attributed to a (then) present-day author rather than a venerated figure from the past.

2. The setting is the (then) present rather than the past.

3. The book is not sealed since the (then) present time is understood to be the end time.

The book of Daniel was written during the persecution under Antiochus Epiphanes (167 B.C.–164 B.C.). However, the book is attributed to Daniel, who lived at the time of the Babylonian Exile (587 B.C.–537 B.C.). Daniel is said to have been told what will occur in the future. However, the "future" events are not future from the point of view of the author. The events have already occurred. Daniel is told to seal up the words of the revelation. "Go your way, Daniel, for the words are to remain secret and sealed until the time of the end" (Dn 12:9). To tell the person who has received the vision to seal up the words until the end time is a convention of the form. The audience, which is contemporary with the author, is reading the sealed vision. Therefore, this convention is used to say that the time of the readers is the end time.

Given this information, it seems wise to elaborate on the answer to two questions to which we have already referred: "Is the author who sets his story in a previous generation and pictures an angel prognosticating 'future events,' when in fact these events have already occurred, misleading his audience?" and "What is meant by the 'end time'? Does this phrase refer to a time in our future?"

The author of apocalyptic literature was not misleading his audience by employing the conventions of apocalyptic literature. Since the author's contemporaries were familiar with these conventions, they would not have been misled. I had an experience recently that illustrated this truth. On December 31, 1994 I was watching a newscast. The reporter said that the "Procrastinators Society of America" had just released its prognostications for 1994. The first prognostication was that "the Pres will cop a doc." Another was that "baseball and hockey will play the same game." The newscaster, with a completely straight face, said that the "Procrastinators Society of America" was very proud of its record for accuracy. Once more their prognostications were 100% accurate.

Since I live in the same society as did the newscaster, I was not misled by this "news report." I realized that the procrastinators had made up their "prognostications" after the events had already occurred. President Clinton had fired the Surgeon General. Baseball players and hockey players had all gone on strike. What was purported to be prognostication was actually the recital of events that had already occurred.

The newscaster reported this story in order to amuse the television audience. The authors of apocalyptic literature had a much more serious purpose in mind by employing the conventions of apocalyptic literature. Their audience was suffering terrible persecution. They were asking, "Where is God? Has God lost control of the course of events?" By picturing an angel telling a person about the course of events, exactly as they are known by the audience to have occurred, the author is expressing the author's belief that God is in control of the course of history. Even such terrible things as persecutions do not inhibit God's power to bring about good. The author is telling his audience to remain faithful to covenant love because the "end time" is near, that is, the time when their present persecution will end.

The "End Time" Not Referring to Our Future

Modern readers often take the words "end time" to mean "the end of the world." Since the world is still here they conclude that the end time has not yet come, and that the events which apocalyptic literature describes are in our future, or even in our present. It is this kind of thinking that causes people to quote the book of Revelation to support their own belief that the end of the world is near.

In fact, the authors of apocalyptic literature were not speaking about a time in our future. In order to understand what the phrase "end time" meant to the authors and audience of apocalyptic literature, we will trace the development of this concept.

The Old Testament prophets often spoke of the "day of the Lord." This phrase was used to refer to the time when God would intervene in the course of events on earth in a definitive way. Originally the phrase referred to the defeat and judgment of Israel's enemies. Because the Israelites understood themselves to be God's chosen people, when they thought of God judging the earth, they thought of God judging Israel's enemies and vindicating Israel. We see this understanding of the "day of the Lord" reflected in Isaiah as he describes what God will do to the Babylonians: "Wail, for the day of the Lord is near; it will come like destruction from the Almighty....See the day of the Lord comes, cruel, with wrath and fierce anger, to make the earth a desolation, and to destroy its sinners from it. For the stars of the heavens and their constellations will not give their light; the sun will be dark at its rising, and the moon will not shed its light. I will punish the world for its evil, and the wicked for their iniquity..." (Is 13:6, 9–11). These words, although they use cosmic imagery, are used to describe God's treatment of Babylon, not of Israel. Israel will not be treated in the same way: "But the Lord will have compassion on Jacob and will again choose Israel, and will set them in their own land; and aliens will join them and attach themselves to the house of Jacob....They will take captive those who were their captors, and rule over those who oppressed them" (Is 14:1–2). This "day of the Lord" would be anticipated with great joy because enemies would be destroyed and Israel would be saved.

However, the prophets pointed out to Israel that God could not tolerate sin. So, if the people are sinning, the "day of the Lord" will mean God's judgment on God's chosen people, not just on foreign enemies. Once this concept was introduced, the "day of the Lord" became a day to be dreaded, not just a day to be looked forward to as a day of vic-

---

**STEP IN THE DEVELOPMENT OF THE
IDEA OF THE "END TIME"**

- The "day of the Lord": the time when God would intervene in events in a definitive way. Israel would be vindicated (Is 13:6, 9–11).

- The "day of the Lord" could mean judgment for the Israelites if they are sinning (Am 5:18, 20).

- The book of Daniel uses apocalyptic images to picture a day or time when the Son of Man will judge the nations (Dn 7:13–14). This "end time" was the time of the original reading audience, a time when their present persecutions would be over.

- This "Son of Man" image is used in the Gospels to describe the "parousia," or the second coming of Jesus (Mt 24:29–31). This coming was expected imminently (Mt 24:34).

tory. As Amos said, "Alas for you who desire the day of the Lord! Why do you want the day of the Lord? It is darkness, not light…. Is not the day of the Lord darkness, not light, and gloom with no brightness in it?" (Am 5:18, 20). The day of the Lord would be darkness for those who failed to act justly, even though they are God's chosen people.

A Son of Man

This idea of a day or a time when God will judge the nations continues in Daniel. Here apocalyptic imagery is used to describe God giving authority to one like "a son of man" who will judge the nations. "I saw one like a son of man coming, on the clouds of heaven; when he reached the Ancient One (i.e. God) and was presented before him, he received dominion, glory, and kingship; nations and peoples of every language serve him. His dominion is an everlasting dominion that shall not be taken away, his kingship shall not be destroyed" (Dn 7:13–14). This passage is offering hope to those who are being persecuted that God will send a messiah, one like a "son of man," to whom God will give power over the Jews' political enemies. Although this decisive intervention on God's part has an "end of the world" tone to it, in that the dominion to be established is to be an "everlasting dominion" that shall never be destroyed, the author is speaking about the defeat of Antiochus Epiphanes. As we have noted, Daniel is told to keep the words secret and the book sealed until "the time of the end" (see Dn 12:4). So the time referred to as the "end time" is the time of the first audience to read the book, the audience who is enduring the persecution.

This "son of man" image is used in the Gospels to describe the "parousia," or the second coming of Jesus. In Matthew we read, "Immediately after the tribulation of those days, the sun will be darkened, and the moon will not give its light, and the stars will fall from the sky, and the powers of the heavens will be shaken. And then the sign of the Son of Man will appear in heaven, and all the tribes of the earth will mourn, and they will see the Son of Man coming upon the clouds of heaven with power and great glory. And he will send out his angels with a trumpet blast, and they will gather his elect from the four winds, from one end of the heavens to the other" (Mt 24:29–31). Here too the apocalyptic imagery is not meant to describe an "end of the world" in our future, but a coming during the time of those who are listening. "Amen, I say to you, this generation will not pass away until all these things have taken place" (Mt 24:34).

By saying that the "end time" refers to the time of the author and audience rather than to a time in our future is not to say that the book of Daniel or the book of Revelation has no application in our lives. These books are in the canon. Their authors were inspired, and the truths they teach are eternal truths which do have an application in our own lives. However, to understand what the eternal truths these books teach are, we will first have to understand what the author is trying to teach his contemporary audience. The revelation which the book contains is tied to the intent of the author.

So far we have explained that the conventions of apocalyptic literature, if misunderstood, could lead us to two erroneous opinions. The first is that the authors of apocalyptic literature claim to be able to prognosticate inevitable future events. This is not the case. Historic events are presented as though they will be future events. The second is that the "end time" to which the authors refer has not yet occurred, and so is in our future. The "end time" to which the authors refer is the time when their audiences first read their works, which were to remain sealed until that "end time."

"Acknowledging" Two Conventions of the Form

Although the book of Revelation does not follow all of the conventions of apocalyptic literature, it does "acknowledge" them. The book of Revelation is not attributed to a venerable person of a past generation. The author of the book identifies himself as John, a contemporary of his persecuted audience. "I, John, your brother, who share with you the distress, the kingdom, and the endurance we have in Jesus, found myself on the island called Patmos because I proclaimed God's word and gave testimony to Jesus" (Rv 1:9). Since John is a contemporary of his reading audience, he does not picture the angel telling him to seal up the book until the end time. Instead he is instructed, "Do not seal up the prophetic words of this book, for the appointed time is near" (Rv 22:10).

Observing the Conventions of the Form

John does observe all of the other conventions of apocalyptic literature. John claims to have had a vision in which he receives a revelation from Christ. He is told to write down "what you have seen, and what is happening, and what will happen afterward" (Rv 1:19). By looking at this first vision of John's, we can illustrate both how the revelation is written in code and why the truth of the revelation is just as essential for our generation as it was for John's.

John describes his vision in these words, "Then I turned to see whose voice it was that spoke to me, and when I turned, I saw seven gold lampstands and in the midst of the lampstands one like a son of man, wearing an ankle-length robe, with a gold sash around his chest. The hair of his head was as white as white wool or as snow, and his eyes were like a fiery flame. His feet were like polished brass refined in a furnace, and his voice was like the sound of rushing water. In his right hand he held seven stars. A sharp two-edged sword came out of his mouth, and his face shone like the sun at its brightest" (Rv 1:12–16).

The Code

To understand both the code and the teaching of this passage, we must turn once again to a passage from Daniel, part of which we just read when we were discussing the image of the "son of man." Daniel is describing a vision he had when he says, "As I watched thrones were set up and the Ancient One took his throne. His clothing was snow bright, and the hair on his head as white as wool; his throne was flames of fire, with wheels of burning fire. A surging stream of fire flowed out from where he sat; thousands upon thousands were ministering to him, and myriads upon myriads attended him....I saw One like a son of man coming, on the clouds of heaven; when he reached the Ancient One and was presented before him, he received dominion, glory, and kingship; nations and peoples of every language serve him. His dominion is an everlasting dominion that shall not be taken away, his kingship shall not be destroyed" (Dn 7:9–10, 13–14).

We already know that the book of Daniel was written during the persecution under Antiochus Epiphanes (167 B.C.–164 B.C.). We also know that, like all apocalyptic literature, this book is offering hope to those who are being persecuted. The hope is based on the belief that God will be faithful to covenant love and so will protect God's people. God will send someone to save those who are being persecuted. This first picture in Daniel 7, then, is a picture of God in God's "throne room." The "ancient one," that is, God, takes the throne. Fire has been a symbol of God's presence throughout the Old Testament. Remember the burning bush. Remember the cloud by day and the fire by night that led the Israelites during the time of the exodus. Thousands upon thousands are ministering to God. This is to say that all of creation is subject to God. God is "in charge." Then, one like a "son of man" comes to the Ancient One and receives from the Ancient One authority over the nations. This is to say that God will send someone to save God's people as God always has. God had sent Moses, David, and Cyrus (the Persian who defeated the Babylonians and let the Israelites return home). God would send someone soon (i.e. the end time is near) to save God's people from Antiochus Epiphanes.

Notice that in the passage from Daniel, the ancient one on the throne and the "son of man" are two distinct figures. However, when we get to the book of Revelation, the "son of man" and the ancient one become the same figure. The "son of man" is the one whose hair is as white as white wool, and whose eyes are like a fiery flame. By combining two images, one an image of God and the other an image of a great and glorious messiah, an image which has become associated with Jesus, the author of the book of Revelation is teaching that Jesus is God. The book of Revelation, like all apocalyptic literature, is offering hope, but now the hope rests on what has been accomplished by Christ's passion, death, and resurrection.

Christology

The book of Revelation is not in the canon because it prognosticates inevitable future events which will precede the end of the world. It is in the canon because of its Christology. It is in the canon because it teaches both who Jesus is and what has been accomplished through Jesus. The fact that Jesus is still in control of events, that Jesus has conquered evil, and that those who remain faithful to Jesus will join him in the heavenly court are taught over and over again in the book of Revelation.

Let us look at another passage that uses code to teach these truths, a passage in which some of the imagery is familiar to us so that it is not so difficult to understand. "Then I saw standing in the midst of the throne and the four living creatures and the elders a Lamb that seemed to have been slain. He had seven horns and seven eyes; these are the seven spirits of God sent out into the whole world. He came and received the scroll from the right hand of the one who sat on the throne. When he took it, the four living creatures and the twenty-four elders fell down before the Lamb. Each of the elders held a harp and gold bowls filled with incense, which are the prayers of the holy one. They sang a new hymn: 'Worthy are you to receive the scroll and to break open its seals, for you were slain and with your blood you purchased for God those from every tribe and tongue, people and nation. You made them a kingdom and priests for our God, and they will reign on earth' " (Rv 5:6–10).

As always in the book of Revelation, we are to "translate" the code into ideas rather than into pictures. The lamb who appears to have been slain is Jesus. The fact that the lamb has seven horns and seven eyes means that Jesus is all-powerful and all-knowing. The number seven signifies perfection. Horns signify strength, and eyes the ability to "see" or to know. The lamb receives the scroll from God. Remember, the scroll contains a hidden revelation known only to God. When it is opened the events which it describes will be precipitated. To ask, "Who is worthy to open the scroll" is to ask "Who has the power to determine the course of history?" Jesus is the only one worthy to open the scroll because Jesus has redeemed the whole human race. So the terrible events which are occurring in the lives of those being persecuted, events described in the plagues, famines, earthquakes, and floods pre-cipitated by the opening of the seals, or the blowing of the trumpets, or the pouring of the bowls, are not signs that God has lost control of his-tory. Rather, God, in the person of the risen Christ, is still in control. The suffering that is occurring is temporary. Those who die are not really dead because their garments have been "washed in the blood of the lamb." Good will finally prevail over evil because, by his passion, death and resurrection, Jesus has conquered evil.

SOME SYMBOLS IN THE BOOK OF REVELATION

On the side of Good

Angel—God's messenger

4—the whole world; a complete number

4 *animals in the heavenly court* (see Ezekiel 1:5—21)—all that is best in the created world

7—completeness

12—completeness

24 elders in heavenly court—the whole Church (12 tribes plus 12 apostles)

Lamb—Christ

Bride—God's people, the Church

Woman—Israel giving birth to the messiah (also Mary and the Church)

Virgins—those who have been faithful; single-hearted

White—purity

White robe washed in blood—apparel of those saved by Christ

Eyes—wisdom

Horns—authority (because powerful)

Long robe—priesthood

Thrones—heavenly court; place where judgment takes place

New Jerusalem—God's redeemed people

On the side of Evil

3 $\frac{1}{2}$ years, 42 months, 1,260 days—short, limited period

666—the evilest one (Nero Caesar)

Dragon—Satan, evil forces

Babylon—not God's people (Rome)

Beast—those who work for evil; Roman officials

Black—death

Scarlet—harlotry, luxury

Sea—opposite of heaven; evil comes from the sea

BOOK OF REVELATION

Setting—Heavenly court.

Action, Events—The action and events proceed from the
heavenly court.

Visions of the Heavenly Court:

1:9–20   The vision which begins here precipitates the
sending of the seven letters.

4:1–11   The vision which begins here precipitates the
opening of the seven seals.

8:2–5   The vision which begins here precipitates the
blowing of the seven trumpets.

12:1–6   The vision which begins here precipitates the
battle between the devil and the woman.

14:1–15:4 The vision which begins here precipitates the
pouring out of the seven bowls.

19:1–10   In this vision the Word goes forth to fight the
final battles.

21:1–8   This vision reveals the final victory of good
over evil.

Conclusion: God has not lost control of events. Good
will conquer evil.

Good News

The book of Revelation is good news because it teaches the saving
power of Jesus to people who desperately need to hear about it. How
is it, then, that passages from the book of Revelation are so often used

to frighten people rather than to reassure them? Obviously, some people use the passages to teach a message different from the message which the original authors intended to teach. We will now look at a few selected passages which are sometimes used to scare people rather than to comfort them. As we did with other passages from the Old and New Testaments, we first will try to name the mistake in interpretation which has resulted in the misunderstanding and then try to offer a correct interpretation.

1. Revelation 6:10; 14:7–20   Scenes of Revenge and Punishment

The Misunderstanding

No one can deny that the book of Revelation contains many scenes of horrible punishment. In chapter 14, an angel who is said to be announcing "good news" (see Rv 14:6) says, "Fear God and give him glory, for his time has come to sit in judgment" (Rv 14:7). Another angel then announces, "Anyone who worships the beast or its image, or accepts its mark on the forehead or hand, will also drink the wine of God's fury, poured full strength into the cup of his wrath, and will be tormented in burning sulfur before the holy angels and before the Lamb. The smoke of the fire that torments them will rise forever and ever, and there will be no relief day or night for those who worship the beast or its image or accept the mark of its name" (Rv 14:9–11).

In addition, the book of Revelation seems to present even those who are already in heaven as calling for revenge on their persecutors. After the fourth seal is broken, John sees "underneath the altar the souls of those who had been slaughtered because of the witness they bore to the word of God. They cried out in a loud voice, 'How long will it be, holy and true master, before you sit in judgment and avenge our blood on the inhabitants of the earth?' " (Rv 6:9–10).

Are such passages teaching the audience that revenge is a good thing and that the Lamb is honored and pleased by the eternal suffering of those who have sinned? Many use such passages to teach just such a lesson.

Why the Error in Interpretation?

The errors in interpretation have their roots in two mistakes. The first is to ignore the ramifications of the genre, to ignore what we know about the audience and the purpose of apocalyptic literature. The second is to misunderstand the images, to presume that apocalyptic literature provides a literal concrete description of events rather than a description of things which are beyond our comprehension.

The Teaching

The teaching behind these passages is supposed to be "good news." Before we hear the descriptions of eternal punishment we are told, "Then I saw another angel flying high overhead, with everlasting good news to announce to those who dwell on earth..." (Rv 14:6). What is the "good news"?

In order to understand the intent behind these passages we will, of course, have to put them in context. As we have said, apocalyptic literature is addressed to those who are suffering persecution. It is purposefully written in code to exclude the persecutors from understanding what has been written. Therefore, we know that passages such as these are not addressed to the persecutors, threatening them with punishment. Rather, the passages are addressed to those who are the victims of persecution. It is good news for the victims of persecution to hear that those who are persecuting them will be overcome and will be held accountable for their actions. The martyrs under the altar who ask "How long?" are not told that judgment will come immediately, but they are told that judgment will come eventually. Those who do evil will not, in the long run, prevail.

In addition, the passages are addressed to those who may be tempted to compromise with the persecutors in order to avoid the terrible suffering that awaits future martyrs. In order to motivate people to fidelity, the book of Revelation pictures the ramifications of infidelity (the eternal fiery pit) as being even worse than the ramifications of fidelity (persecution and possible martyrdom). The "second death," God's judgment on those who compromise with their Roman persecutors (i.e. bear the mark of the beast), is pictured as far worse than the first death, the death inflicted by the persecutors. The first death leads to eternal life.

So the intent behind such passages is not to give a literal description of the fate of the persecutors. It is to assure the persecuted that God has power over evil, that evil has already been defeated by Christ. Additionally, such passages are intended to motivate the faint of heart to continue to be faithful under the most difficult of circumstances. That the passage is intended to motivate people to fidelity is explicitly stated, "Here is what sustains the holy ones who keep God's commandments and their faith in Jesus" (Rv 14:12).

2. Revelation 7:1–8; 14:1–5   Will only 144,000 make it to heaven?

The Misunderstanding

Many years ago two missionaries knocked on my front door, wanting to come in and tell me about their beliefs. Among the ideas they shared with me was their belief that only 144,000 people would make it to heaven. They based this belief on their understanding of the following passages: "Then I saw another angel come up from the East, holding the seal of the living God. He cried out in a loud voice to the four angels who were given power to damage the land and the sea, 'Do not damage the land or the sea or the trees until we put the seal on the foreheads of the servants of our God.' I heard the number of those who had been marked with the seal, one hundred and forty-four thousand marked..." (Rv 7:2–4). "Then I looked and there was the Lamb on Mount Zion, and with him a hundred and forty-four thousand who had his name and his Father's name written on their foreheads....They were singing what seemed to be a new hymn before the throne, before the four living creatures and the elders. No one could learn this hymn except the hundred and forty-four thousand who had been ransomed from the earth" (Rv 14:1, 3). My visitors explained to me that this scene was picturing the "end of the world" (yet to come), and that it was crucial that I convert promptly so that I might be one of the 144,000 to be saved.

To this day I am in awe of the generosity of those missionaries. If I shared their belief that only 144,000 would be saved, I do not think that I would be so generous as to stir up the competition for the remaining spots. I think that those missionaries will have a high place in heaven, and that they will be absolutely amazed at how many others are in heaven, too.

Why the Error in Interpretation?

The error in interpretation, again, results from two misunderstandings: The first is the presumption that the phrase "end time" refers to a future end of the world rather than to the end of the persecution which the original audience is suffering. The second is a lack of knowledge about the way in which numbers are used in apocalyptic literature. Since we already discussed the meaning of the phrase "end time" in apocalyptic literature earlier in this chapter, we need here only address the use of numbers in apocalyptic literature.

The Teaching

In the book of Revelation, numbers are used symbolically. There are two categories of numbers, those that represent completeness and those that represent incompleteness. Some numbers that represent completeness include twelve and one thousand. The number twelve recalls both the twelve tribes and the twelve apostles. The number one thousand represents fullness. The number one hundred forty-four thousand is also one of the numbers which represents completeness because it is a

---

NUMBERS WHICH SYMBOLIZE COMPLETENESS

4 The whole world

7 Used in basic structure of book and of sequences

12 Completeness (tribes, apostles)

24 Tribes plus apostles

multiple of twelve and one thousand (12 x 12 x 1,000 = 144,000). Therefore, since 144,000 represents the multiplication of completeness, it is not intended to represent a distinct and limited number. Rather it represents an immense number, the whole Church.

In addition to the fact that 144,000 represents a great number, the 144,000 who are sealed are not the only ones who appear in heaven. As the vision continues John says, "After this I had a vision of a great multitude, which no one could count, from every nation, race, people, and tongue. They stood before the throne and before the Lamb, wearing white robes and holding palm branches in their hands. They cried out in a loud voice: 'Salvation comes from our God...' " (Rv 7:9–10). The good news in the book of Revelation is that there is room in heaven for everyone. A great multitude from every nation has been saved by the blood of the Lamb.

3. Revelation 13:1–18   Who is 666?

The Misunderstanding

In popular culture "666" stands for the antichrist. Those who think that the book of Revelation is describing specific events in our future try to find people in our generation who they think might be the antichrist and therefore can be designated "666." Some people consider the Pope to be "666." I have also read that some consider the leader of the "Moonies" to be "666." Some people even think Ronald Reagan is "666" because they disagree with his thinking and each of his three names contains six letters. Such interpretations do nothing more than reveal the prejudices of those who try to assign the "666" label. These interpretations in no way enable us to understand the truths about God which the book of Revelation contains.

Why the Error in Interpretation?

As was true with the misinterpretation of "144,000" saved, the errors in interpretation of "666" result from two misunderstandings about apocalyptic literature. The first is to presume that the function of this kind of writing is to speak of a time in our future rather than to speak of the end of the contemporary audience's present persecution. The second is to misunderstand the way in which numbers are used in apocalyptic literature. Again, since the first mistake has already been addressed, we need only discuss in more detail the use of numbers in apocalyptic literature, in this case numbers which represent incompleteness.

The Teaching

Just as some numbers represent completeness, so other numbers represent incompleteness. The number six represents incompleteness for two reasons. First, it is half of twelve, a number which we have already seen represents completeness. Second, six is one less than seven, another number which represents completeness. Numbers which represent incompleteness are used to describe that which is internally flawed, which cannot last, or which is evil. So to refer to someone with a six is to say both that the person is evil and that the person will not prevail. To repeat something three times is to make it superlative. To say that God is "holy, holy, holy" is to say that God is most holy. To name someone "666" is to say that this person is most evil.

In the book of Revelation the author says, "Wisdom is needed here; one who understands can calculate the number of the beast, for it is a number that stands for a person. His number is six hundred and sixty-six" (Rv 13:18) This passage follows the description of two beasts. The first beast is from the sea and has ten horns and seven heads. This beast

---

NUMBERS WHICH SYMBOLIZE INCOMPLETENESS

$1/4$ of earth
$1/3$ of earth
Any fraction
$3^1/_2$ years
42 months (same as $3^1/_2$ years)
1,260 days (same as $3^1/_2$ years)
666 the superlative evil

represents the Roman Empire, which is persecuting John's contemporaries. The individual heads on the beast represent individual emperors. The second beast also represents the Roman Empire, but on the level of local leaders who speak for the emperor. The second beast wields "all the authority of the first beast in its sight and made the earth and its inhabitants worship the first beast…" (Rv 13:12).

The beast referred to as "666" is Nero Caesar, a Roman emperor who had inflicted terrible persecutions on Christians. Hebrew letters had quantitative value, and the sum of the letters which made up the name Nero Caesar was 666. However, since 666 names the superlative of evil, as time has passed it has become a symbol for any great evil that opposes Christ and Christ's Church. When we use "666" to name present evils that oppose the Church, we are using an image from the book of Revelation to refer to events of our own day. But the intent of the author of the book of Revelation was not to prognosticate specific events and people in our future. The intent, as the author made clear by writing in the form of apocalyptic literature, was to address a message of hope to his own contemporaries.

4. Revelation 17:1–18   Who is the whore of Babylon?

The Misunderstanding

In some anti-Catholic tracts, the Pope is understood to be the whore of Babylon. Those who are prejudiced against the Roman Catholic Church make such an interpretation because they realize that within the book of Revelation the whore is associated with Rome. Since Rome is the location of the Pope, they erroneously conclude that the author of the book of Revelation is speaking of the Pope when he condemns the whore of Babylon.

Why the Error in Interpretation?

The error in interpretation results from removing the book's symbolic reference to Rome from the historical setting of John and his

audience, and misapplying it to an altogether different historical setting. This mistake, of course, is again the result of simply not knowing
anything about the form "apocalyptic" literature. A person misunderstands apocalyptic literature whenever he or she presumes that the
intent of the author of the book of Revelation is to speak about specific
events or people in a generation other than his own.

The Teaching

There can be no doubt that the whore of Babylon and the beast
upon which she sits represent the Roman Empire. "...I saw a woman
seated on a scarlet beast that was covered with blasphemous names,
with seven heads and ten horns. The woman was wearing purple and
scarlet and adorned with gold, precious stones, and pearls. She held
in her hand a gold cup that was filled with the abominable and sordid
deeds of her harlotry. On her forehead was written a name, which is
a mystery, 'Babylon the great, the mother of harlots and of the abominations of the earth.' I saw that the woman was drunk on the blood
of the holy ones and on the blood of the witnesses to Jesus" (Rv
17:3–6).

The beast upon which the harlot sits is the same beast that we just
discussed in the passage with 666. We recognize it by its seven heads
and ten horns. The harlot is named Babylon. Babylon is used as a code
for Rome because Babylon had conquered Jerusalem in 587 B.C. and
had destroyed the temple. Rome, too, has now conquered Jerusalem
and has destroyed the rebuilt temple. The harlot is drunk on the blood
of the martyrs. It is Rome which has been killing Christians. The
decadence and luxury associated with Rome are clearly visible in the
description of the harlot. That the harlot represents the Roman Empire
at the time when the book of Revelation was written is clearly stated.
"The woman whom you saw represents the great city that has sover-
eignty over the kings of the earth" (Rv 17:18). Because Rome
(Babylon) has become an instrument of evil, the author of the book of
Revelation knows that Rome will fall. Christ has already defeated
evil.

Eternal Truths Taught in the Book of Revelation

Because apocalyptic literature, by definition, is offering assurance to an audience contemporary with the author that the "end time," the end of the present persecution, is imminent, we have insisted that any interpretation that takes the phrase "end time" to refer to a time in our future is a misinterpretation. Are we then saying that the book of Revelation has no relevance for our generation or for future generations?

Of course not. By the fact that this particular work of apocalyptic literature has been accepted as part of the canon, the Christian community claims that the book teaches eternal truths. What then are the eternal truths which the book of Revelation teaches? We have named these truths in the course of explaining the teaching behind various passages. Here we simply summarize what has already been illustrated.

ETERNAL TRUTHS TAUGHT IN THE BOOK OF REVELATION

- Only God should be worshiped.
- The risen Christ is God. Christ has a cosmic role.
- Through his passion, death and resurrection Christ has redeemed humankind.
- The risen Christ is judge. Good will be rewarded. Evil will be punished.
- The martyrs are already with Christ in heaven.
- Those suffering persecution should persevere in hope. To choose "death" is to choose life. Christ will save.

The book of Revelation teaches that Jesus Christ is God. The book contains a "high Christology," that is, it attributes a cosmic role to Christ. Christ already reigns in heaven. All events that occur within the book of Revelation are precipitated by actions of the lamb who is already victorious in heaven. Jesus' cosmic role is clearly stated when Jesus is pictured as saying, "I am the Alpha and the Omega, the first and the last, the beginning and the end" (Rv 22:13).

The book of Revelation also teaches that only God should be worshiped. This teaching against idolatry is central to the function of prophecy and it permeates the book of Revelation. Those who worship the beast face condemnation. Even John, when he fell down to worship the angel, is reminded that only God should be worshiped. The angel says, "Don't! I am a fellow servant of yours and of your brothers the prophets and of those who keep the message of this book. Worship God" (Rv 22:9).

Also central to the book's teaching is the redemptive power of Jesus' passion, death, and resurrection. All the references to the martyrs who are in heaven because their garments have been washed in the blood of the lamb are claims of the redemptive power of Christ's passion, death, and resurrection. The very theme of the book, "Remain faithful to Christ and persevere even if it means martyrdom," rests on the belief that those who die with Christ will rise with Christ. The glorious destiny of those who remain faithful is described in the picture of the new Jerusalem. "Blessed are they who wash their robes so as to have the right to the tree of life and enter the city through its gates" (Rv 22:14).

The only bad news in the book of Revelation is for the persecutors, for the book says that sinners who refuse to repent will suffer "the second death." To the intended audience, those who are suffering persecution, this is good news. Those doing the persecuting will ultimately be defeated. Typical apocalyptic imagery of unending fire and torture is used to describe the fate of persecutors and unrepentant sinners.

We see, then, that in the book of Revelation, as in every book of the Bible, the core message is that God is love and that God will remain faithful to the covenant with God's people. Also, the book makes clear that it is not God's will for anyone to remain an unrepentant sinner. Even as he describes the suffering of those who reject Christ, the author emphasizes the fact that it is God's will that everyone, even the persecutors, respond to the call to repent and live in union with God. "The Spirit and the bride say, 'Come.' Let the hearer say, 'Come.' Let the one who thirsts come forward, and the one who wants it receive the gift of life-giving water" (Rv 22:17). If God had God's way, all would come to the water and live in covenant love.

Chapter 4
God Loves and Saves

The core revelation of Scripture, both Old and New Testaments, is that God is love. Why, then, are so many of us unable to believe this good news? Why do religious figures sometimes preach a God of hell and damnation? Why are many of us taught that we must earn God's love? Why do we fear God? Why do we fail to trust God's loving providence?

To some extent, the answer to these questions is that we misunderstand what we read in Scripture. As we already know, Scripture reveals a two thousand year process of people growing in their knowledge of God. We have seen that inspired authors came to realize the ramifications of the good news of God's love gradually. For instance, in teaching that God will love and protect God's people, inspired authors did not always realize or keep in mind that God loves everyone. They pictured God as loving and protecting them, but as hating and destroying their enemies. We have already noted passages that reveal this point of view in Chapter 2 when we discussed "the ban" (see Dt 7:1–11), and in Chapter 3 when we discussed the scenes of revenge and punishment in the book of Revelation (see Rv 6:10; 14:7–20). Those who are not able to understand the intent of the author in such passages, who are not able to separate the eternal truth which the author is teaching from the author's presumptions, often misunderstand the revelation. They think that Scripture itself reveals a God who fails to forgive, who fails to love.

In Chapters 2 and 3 we have tried to correct such misinterpretations both by explaining the reason for the mistake in interpretation and by offering a correct interpretation. The task in this chapter is to reaffirm

115

the core teaching of Scripture, that God is love, by examining just a few of the many passages which explicitly teach it. We will see that Scripture clearly teaches us that God is love, that God always forgives, and that God offers salvation to everyone. It is because God always loves and always forgives that we are required to do the same.

I have often heard Christians say that the New Testament teaches a God of love, but the Old Testament teaches a God of vengeance. This statement is not true. Both the Old and New Testaments teach a God of love. The very word "testament" helps us understand this fact. "Testament" means "covenant." The central metaphor to describe the loving relationship between God and God's people in both the Old and New Testaments is "covenant." The word "covenant," by definition, refers to the belief that God has entered into a permanent relationship of love with us which cannot be broken even in the face of our infidelity. The reason why covenant love cannot be broken is that God cannot stop loving. It is against God's nature to stop loving. It is impossible because God is love. The whole Old Testament is an account of the Israelites' experience of covenant love.

None of the present Old Testament reached the form in which we now have it until after the experience of the Exodus. A belief in God's covenant love did precede the experience of the Exodus, but the accounts of God forming a covenant with the patriarchs, with Abraham, Isaac, Jacob, and Joseph, are told through the lens of the Exodus experience. The Exodus was an experience of God's saving power and of God keeping God's promises. The Hebrews understood God to have bent down and obligated God's self by promising Abraham and Abraham's descendants land and protection. God's only motive for doing this was love. The escape from Egypt, the protection in the desert with water, manna, and quail, and the establishment of the nation under King David were all understood as examples of God keeping God's promises, as examples of God's covenant love.

Imagine for a moment that you had been alive at the time of the Exodus. You would have had no Old Testament to read. However, you would have heard the stories of your ancestors' relationship with God. You would have heard of the promises which offered hope, even as you lived in slavery in Egypt. Imagine how you would have felt as Moses rallied the people, as events unfolded allowing you actually to escape from your slavery, as you found food and water in the desert. It was all true! God is powerful and present! God does save! God does love us! From then on you would interpret all events, good and bad, in the light of this overwhelming experience of God's saving power.

Years ago I gained an appreciation for how an experience of God's saving power can become the lens through which one sees all of life's events. It was obviously insignificant compared to the Exodus, but it was a marvelous act of God to me. This event occurred in 1978 when it was time for me to take my doctoral comprehensives for a Ph.D. in English literature. I was petrified. At the University of Kentucky I was required to select three areas in which to be examined. I selected medieval literature, renaissance literature, and nineteenth century literature.

As I began my preparations I felt completely overwhelmed by the quantity of material. I went to the Chair of the department to explain my situation. I told him that I had completed my bachelor's degree eighteen years earlier and had been working slowly on my master's and Ph.D., taking a course every semester as my husband, Don, and I raised our four children. In addition, we had moved several times so my course work had been done at three different universities. I asked if I could have a reading list so that I could focus my studies on those works which might appear on the exams.

His answer is ingrained in my memory: "There is no reading list. If it is written in English it may be on the test."

As I returned home I was considering whether or not I should even try to take the test under these circumstances. Two things I had read came to mind. One was a comment I read by Chesterton: "Anything worth doing is worth doing poorly." The second was the parable of the talents which I had taught many times (see Mt 25:14–30). This parable is part of a sermon which Jesus is pictured as giving to his disciples about the end times. The message is, "Do not, in this 'in-between time,' let fear of failure prevent you from using your 'talents' in service to the master." I decided to prepare for the tests rather than to choose failure by being afraid to take them.

For nine months giving me time to study became a family project. We had a work chart that divided up household duties among all the members of the family. This gave me time to study eight hours a day, during which time I went over all the works and all the notes I had taken since I started college in 1959.

The first of the three tests, on medieval literature, was on Easter Monday. On Good Friday I was sitting in church not listening to the sermon when it occurred to me that sermons are a form of medieval literature, and I knew very little about them. In the parking lot after the service I mentioned this to my husband. He said, "You go to the library and get something on medieval sermons. I'll take the kids home." The rest of Good Friday and Holy Saturday I spent reading the book I had found in the library. On Easter Sunday I was going through some Chaucer notes which I had taken as an undergraduate when I noticed a section entitled, "the form of a medieval sermon compared to Chaucer's *Pardoner's Tale.*" It applied the form of a medieval sermon to this particular story.

On Easter Monday I sat down to take the test on medieval literature. One question, on which we were supposed to spend an hour, one third of the test, was, "Write on the medieval sermonizing techniques in the *Friar's* and *Pardoner's Tale.*" I knew I could do a good job on that one.

As soon as I got home I told my husband exactly what had happened. We talked over the best way for me to spend the next day, Tuesday, in preparation for Wednesday's test on renaissance literature. My husband said, "Don't review all your notes on all those plays. If you do you'll get the plots and characters mixed up. Just pick one book on one topic and read it to keep your mind occupied."

I decided to read a book which a friend had handed me weeks earlier, entitled *Spenser's Faerie Queene: Continued Allegory or Dark Conceit.* By Tuesday night I had taken six pages of notes on that book.

The next day one of the questions was to write for ninety minutes, one half of the test, on "allegory in the *Faerie Queene.*" Before I wrote my answer, I knelt down (I was alone in the room) and said a prayer of gratitude. I believed then, and I believe now, that my own efforts were not sufficient for me to pass the test. God "arranged things" so that I did pass, and I am very, very grateful. I am grateful not only to have passed the comprehensives, but even more to have had a personal experience of God's saving power. Ever since then, I have thought that I understand the Exodus experience better, and that I know why the Israelites continued to believe in God's love, presence, and saving power even when things were not going their way. Once a person or a nation has had such an experience, it is never forgotten. All subsequent experiences are interpreted in the light of that experience, not only "good fortune," but "bad fortune," not only open doors, but closed doors. Nothing that happens is seen as happening outside the providence of a loving God.

So the "interpretive lens" of all that is recounted in Scripture is a personal experience of God's love. The Old Testament is an interpretation of events that preceded Jesus Christ in the context of God's covenant love. The New Testament is an interpretation of events that revolved around Jesus Christ in the context of God's covenant love. The very name of the collections tells us that we will understand what we read only if we see it all in the context of God's love for God's people. We will now look at passages in the Old Testament which teach of God's love.

OLD TESTAMENT PASSAGES

1. Genesis 1:1–2:4   Created in God's image

Our religious tradition has put a good deal of emphasis on "original sin." For some reason we have lost track of the fact that the story of our origins with which Scripture begins is not about original sin. It is about original goodness. It is about how God made us for no motive other than love, and how God looked at all that God had created and found it "very good." In order to fully appreciate the good news contained in this story, we will have to interpret the story as contextualists.

The first question a contextualist asks is, "What is the literary form of the story?" The creation story, like the story of the man and woman in the garden which we have already discussed, is a myth. In other words, it is an imaginative and symbolic story about a reality beyond our comprehension. In this instance the reality is the fact that we and all the rest of creation exist. The story is an imaginative response to the inspired author's question, "Why?" Why do we exist? What is our origin and our purpose? The function of the story is to orient us in a moral universe.

The author of the creation story lived in a time before science. He presumed that the earth was flat and had a solid dome over it. He believed that there were holes in the dome through which the water above the dome could reach the land beneath. The author was not trying to explain the origins of the earth from a scientific point of view. Rather, he was trying to explain the relationship of the whole created order to the loving God who created it.

So the author imagines a time before creation when God's "wind" hovered over the waters. The author pictures God creating everything that exists simply through the power of God's word. God says, "Let there be…." And there it was. To structure his story the author picks a workweek. This structure reinforces his theme that creation is God's work, but it also reveals that the time of the author and the time of the plot of the story are not the same. This is not an ancient story that dates to the earliest days of civilization. Rather, this is a story written by someone in a well-developed society that was itself organized by a workweek.

In fact, Scripture scholars believe that this story dates to around 450 B.C., after the Israelites had returned from their exile in Babylon. The story is teaching traditional beliefs that had been challenged by the beliefs of the Babylonians. The Babylonians believed in many gods. This story reinforces the traditional Jewish belief in one God. The Babylonians regarded the sun and moon as gods. This story teaches that the sun and moon are material creations. Far from controlling human beings, the sun and the moon serve human beings by providing light. The Babylonians believed that spirit was good but that matter was not. The Jews did not agree with this dualism. This story expresses the Jewish belief that since God made all that exists, all that exists must be good. This truth is emphasized over and over. After each day God looks at what God has created and pronounces it "good."

However, the greatest difference between the beliefs of the Babylonians and the beliefs of the Jews was in their view of human nature. The Babylonians thought of human nature as being flawed at its core. This belief was expressed by the Babylonians in their creation story, which pictured gods creating human beings out of the corpse of a rebellious, defeated god. The Jews, on the other hand, think of human beings as being good at their core. God is pictured as creating both male and female in God's own image. God gives human beings dominion over creation and blesses them. This dominion is to be exercised as God exercises dominion, not by destroying but by creating, by giving life. God tells human beings to be fruitful. God trusts human beings to take good care of all the rest of creation. After completing all of creation God looks at all that has been created and calls it "very good."

Not only does God create human beings in God's own image, but God establishes a way for human beings to continue to think about, treasure, and celebrate their relationship with God. God blesses the seventh day and hallows it. Scripture scholars think that this picture of even God observing the sabbath was the author's way of reemphasizing the importance of observing the sabbath to those who had returned

---

MYTH: An Imaginative and Symbolic Story About a Reality Which Is Beyond Comprehension

Function: To orient people in a moral universe

Creation Story

Three days of separation	*Three days of population*
• Light/Darkness	• Sun, Moon, Stars
• Water (firmament) / water	• Birds, Fish
• Water/Dry Land	• Animals, Human beings

Story Teaches: –There is one God
– All creation is good, especially human beings
– Sun and moon are not gods
– Human beings are made in the image of a loving God

---

from exile. While in exile the Israelites were without their temple. Some of the religious traditions which they had observed in the holy land undoubtedly had fallen by the wayside. On their return the priests reedited the whole tradition of the people from the time of Abraham. In retelling the story, the priests emphasized the importance of observing the sabbath and of worshiping in the second, newly built temple. As part of their editing of the traditions, they placed this story of creation at the beginning of the whole narrative. In doing so they emphasized God's love and the blessed state of human beings. God's love and blessing thus became, and remain, the beginning of the story.

2. Hosea 2:16–20; 11:1–4, 8–9   God as a loving spouse and parent

As we discussed in Chapter 3, the context in which a prophet spoke for God was the context of covenant love. Because God loves, God cannot allow sin to continue or prevail without disastrous consequences. Because God loves, God's people should never give up hope. God will save. No prophet spoke more poignantly of God's unfailing love than did the prophet Hosea. Hosea prophesied to the Northern Kingdom during the reign of Jeroboam II (786–746 B.C.).

Hosea had the great misfortune of being married to an unfaithful wife. In Hosea's culture, a person need not have been saddled on and on with such a terrible problem. The law allowed adulteresses to be stoned to death. However, Hosea could not bring himself to inflict this punishment on his unfaithful wife. As he meditated on the reason behind his unwillingness to condemn her, Hosea began to realize that he and his wife were a living metaphor for the relationship between Yahweh and Israel. Yahweh, too, was "married" to an unfaithful spouse. Yahweh too could destroy the unfaithful spouse but did not want to.

Hosea pictures God trying to win back God's faithless wife with these beautiful words: "Therefore, I will now allure her, and bring her into the wilderness, and speak tenderly to her. From there I will give her her vineyards, and make the Valley of Achor a door of hope. There she shall respond as in the days of her youth, as at the time when she came out of the land of Egypt. On that day, says the Lord, you will call me, 'My husband,' and no longer will you call me, 'My Baal.' For I will remove the names of the Baals from her mouth, and they shall be mentioned by name no more. I will make for you a covenant on that day with the wild animals, the birds of the air, and the creeping things of the ground; and I will abolish the bow, the sword, and war from the land; and I will make you lie down in safety. And I will take you for my wife forever; I will take you for my wife in righteousness and in justice, in steadfast love and in mercy. I will take you for my wife in faithfulness; and you shall know the Lord" (Hos 2:16–20).

In addition to using the metaphor of a husband's love for his wife to describe God's love for Israel, Hosea uses the metaphor of a parent's love for a child. In this tender passage, the Northern Kingdom is referred to by the name of one of its tribes, Ephraim. Again, the point is that God continues to love even when God's love is unrequited. "When Israel was a child, I loved him, and out of Egypt I called my son. The more I called them, the more they went from me; they kept sacrificing to the Baals, and offering incense to idols. Yet it was I who taught Ephraim to walk. I took them up in my arms; but they did not know that I healed them. I led them with cords of human kindness, with bands of love. I was to them like those who lift infants to their cheeks. I bent down to them and fed them....How can I give you up, Ephraim? How can I hand you over, O Israel? How can I make you like Admah? How can I treat you like Zeboim? My heart recoils within me; my compassion grows warm and tender. I will not execute my fierce anger; I will not again destroy Ephraim; for I am God and no mortal, the Holy One in your midst, and I will not come in wrath" (Hos 11:1–4, 8–9)

The prophet pictures God refraining from destroying the people, but not because they deserve to be spared. God recoils from destroying the people because God is love.

3. Isaiah 54:1–10   God's steadfast love will never depart

The book of Isaiah contains the work of three prophets from three separate times in history. Chapters 40–55 make up a section which Scripture scholars refer to as Second Isaiah or Deutero-Isaiah. This prophet lived toward the end of the Babylonian Exile. The people had suffered terribly from the loss of their kingdom and their temple. Second Isaiah was a prophet of hope, encouraging the people to maintain their belief in covenant love and their belief that God would bring good out of their terrible suffering.

Second Isaiah pictures God assuring the people that even though they have suffered, they are still God's people and God still loves them. "For a brief moment I abandoned you, but with great compassion I will gather you. In overflowing wrath for a moment I hid my face from you, but with everlasting love I will have compassion on you, says the Lord, your Redeemer. This is like the days of Noah to me. Just as I swore that the waters of Noah would never again go over the earth, I have sworn that I will not be angry with you and will not rebuke you. For the mountains may depart and the hills be removed, but my steadfast love shall not depart from you, and my covenant of peace shall not be removed, says the Lord, who has compassion on you" (Is 54:7–10).

In the face of the most terrible suffering which the nation had endured since their slavery in Egypt, Second Isaiah was able to preach hope because he understood the ramifications of covenant love. Since God is love, God cannot stop loving, and will therefore save and protect God's people.

4. Jonah   God loves even our enemies

Jesus taught us that we should love our enemies. In Matthew's Gospel, Jesus is pictured as saying, "You have heard that it was said, 'You shall love your neighbor and hate your enemy.' But I say to you, Love your enemies and pray for those who persecute you, so that you may be children of your Father in heaven; for he makes his sun rise on the evil and on the good, and sends rain on the righteous and on the unrighteous" (Mt 5:43–45). We can't turn to a single Old Testament passage which says, "Hate your enemy." But, as we have already seen, we can turn to a number of passages, both Old and New Testament, which presume that it is all right to hate an enemy. Psalm 58 is still another example: "The righteous will rejoice when they see vengeance done; they will bathe their feet in the blood of the wicked. People will say, 'Surely there is a reward for the righteous; surely there is a God who judges on earth' " (Ps 58:10–11). The author of this Psalm would not have been able to grasp the message, "Love your enemy."

However, another Old Testament author did understand that God loves even the enemies of God's chosen people. This courageous person is the author of the book of Jonah. He lived after the Babylonian Exile, an exile that ended because Cyrus, a Persian, conquered the Babylonians and let the Israelites return to their own land. What an amazing event! The Israelites always did expect God to send someone to save them when they were defeated or persecuted. The idea that God would protect and save is core to covenant love. However, the expectation was always that God would raise up one of their own to save them. Moses had been God's instrument of salvation from the Egyptians. Although Moses had been raised as an Egyptian, he was actually an Israelite. David had been God's instrument of salvation from the Philistines. After the time of David, the "savior" or "messiah" who was to come was always compared to David. "One like David" would be God's instrument to defeat their enemies and restore peace. However, their "savior" turned out to be Cyrus, a Persian. The author of Jonah must have reflected on this event at great length. The unavoidable fact was that God had used someone from a nation other than Israel to rescue the Israelites from the hands of their enemies. This meant that God loved other nations too, a very threatening conclusion.

How might the inspired author pass on this threatening truth to a resistant audience? He chooses a teaching tool perfect for his purposes: satiric fiction. He pictures God calling a prophet, Jonah, to preach to a city that no longer exists at the time the author is writing (450 B.C.) but which had been Israel's arch-enemy, Nineveh. Nineveh had been the capital of Assyria, the nation which had conquered the Northern Kingdom in 721 B.C. So the Ninevites function as a symbol for "the enemy."

Jonah, like all prophets, resists his call, but not because he does not speak well or because he is too young or because he is not worthy. Jonah does not want to preach to the Ninevites because he does not want them to be saved. In fact, when the Ninevites, from the king to the cows, repent and dress in sackcloth and ashes, Jonah is disgusted. His worst fears have come true. A compassionate and forgiving God is going to spare the enemy! Jonah's petty personality prevails as he goes out to the desert to pout. However, God cares about Jonah, too, and tries to help Jonah understand why God loves even the Ninevites. God destroys a plant which had given Jonah shade. When Jonah complains, God says, "You are concerned about the bush, for which you did not labor and which you did not grow; it came into being in a night and perished in a night. And should I not be concerned about Nineveh, that great city, in which there are more than a hundred and twenty thousand persons who do not know their right hand from their left, and also many animals?" (Jon 4:10–11).

God loves the Ninevites because God made them, just as God made every single person on earth. The Ninevites, enemy or not, are still God's children. Through his satiric humor the author of Jonah is teach-

A PROCESS OF REVELATION

Coming to Knowledge by Reflecting on Experience

Question: Whom does God love?

Date	Understanding
1850 B.C.	Abraham understood that God is a personal and loving God. God especially loved Abraham. God promised him protection, land, and descendants.
1250 B.C.	The Hebrews understood that God was a personal and loving God. God especially loved the Hebrew people, and freed them from slavery in Egypt.
1200–1000 B.C.	The Israelites understood that God loved them. God helped them conquer Canaan.
537 B.C.	Cyrus, a Persian, conquered the Babylonians and let the Israelites return home.
500–400 B.C.	The author of Jonah understood that God must love other nations. After all, God created them just as God created the Jewish people.
30 A.D.	Jesus taught his followers to love their enemies.
34 A.D.	Peter understood that all people are invited to be God's chosen people and live in a convenant relationship with their God.

ing his fellow Jews that God loves even their enemies. If God loves the Israelites' enemies, are not God's chosen people required to love their enemies too? It is this insight which Jesus handed on to his disciples, a hard truth based on the revelation taught some four hundred years earlier by the author of the book of Jonah.

NEW TESTAMENT PASSAGES

5. Romans 1:16–17; 5:6–11   God's justice is God's saving power

The biblical authors who assume that their enemies are also God's enemies feel justified in calling for the destruction of those who have harmed them because they view the destruction of their enemies as the act of a just God. However, the idea that God's "justice" means that each person gets what that person deserves is challenged over and over again in the New Testament. In fact, none of us, neither our enemies nor ourselves, get exactly what we deserve. We all get many more blessings than we deserve.

Paul, in his letter to the Romans, tells us that God's "justice" is revealed by God's power to save. In the passage which we will read, translations differ in whether they use the word "justice," "righteousness," or "uprightness." In the Latin, the original Greek is translated as *justitia Dei.* Perhaps "righteousness" is preferred over "justice" in some translations for the very reason which we are discussing. When English speaking readers see the word "justice" attributed to God, we think of a God who distributes just punishments, not of a God who saves sinners.

In his letter to the Romans, Paul says this about God's "justice": "For I am not ashamed of the Gospel: it is the power of God for salvation, to everyone who has faith, to the Jews first and also the Greeks. For in it the justice (righteousness) of God is revealed through faith for faith; as it is written, 'He who through faith is just (righteous) shall live' " (Rom 1:16–17).

What attribute of God is being named when Paul refers to "the justice of God"? Here God's "justice" is revealed by God's power to save.

Sometimes the English word "justice" is used to describe giving out "just punishments." When "justice" is associated with giving out just punishments, justice seems to be in opposition to mercy. When we limit the word "justice" to this sense we have the idea that God cannot be just and merciful at the same time. God must choose between these two attributes.

However, we also use the word "just" in a slightly different sense. We say that something is "just right." Here we mean that something is as it should be. In this sense we might describe a level wall as "just," or a well balanced artistic arrangement as "just."

When the letter to the Romans refers to God's "justice" or "righteousness" the word is used in this second sense. Paul is speaking of a quality of God which is just as it should be since God is God. God's "justice" is God's saving power. Because God is love God is acting just like God when God is saving, not when God is punishing. For Paul, a just God is a God who acquits us of our sin.

Paul goes on to marvel at the fact that God reconciled us to God's self not after we repented but while we were still sinners. Paul says, "But God proves his love for us in that while we were still sinners Christ died for us. How much more then, since we are now justified by his blood, will we be saved through him from the wrath. Indeed, if, while we were enemies, we were reconciled to God through the death of his Son, how much more, once reconciled, will we be saved by his life" (Rom 5:8–10). We did not earn salvation by our good behavior. A "just" God has not treated us as we deserve. A "just" God has saved us even though we do not deserve it.

6. Matthew 20:1–16   Salvation is a gift

Paul, of course, learned what he learned about the love of God because of the revelation of God's love which we have all received through Jesus Christ. Jesus, too, taught his disciples that God's love is extravagant and unearned. Jesus tried to make this clear to the disciples, and especially to Peter, when he told them the parable of the vineyard workers.

As we already know from Chapter 2, a parable is the middle of a conversation. To understand what is being taught through a parable we need to ask ourselves to whom Jesus is speaking, and why he told the parable to this particular person. Matthew's Gospel pictures Jesus telling the parable of the vineyard laborers to Peter and the other disciples as part of a long sermon about the end times. Peter has said to Jesus, "Look, we have left everything and followed you. What then will we have?" (Mt 19:27). It is in response to this question that Jesus tells the parable. Behind the question Jesus can hear a misunderstanding on Peter's part, one which many of us share, that he is somehow earning God's love and God's gifts.

Jesus tells Peter that the kingdom of God is like a landowner who goes out early to hire workers for his vineyard. The first workers who are hired agree to work all day for the usual daily wage. Later the landowner hires more workers, and still later he hires even more workers. When the day's work is over the landowner pays the workers in the opposite order than he hired them, and he pays those who worked just a short time the same daily wage which he had promised to those whom he had hired first. The workers who had labored all day observe this and conclude that they will be paid more than was originally agreed upon. However, the landowner pays them just what he paid those who worked less. The all-day workers become angry and complain to the landowner. In response, the landowner points out that they have received what they earned so they have no cause to be angry— unless, of course, they are angry because the landowner is generous.

I know from teaching this parable over the years that many of us react to the parable just as the laborers who worked all day react. We bring to it the presumption that people should get only what they earn. Of course, like the all-day workers, we see nothing wrong with people being overly generous to us, but we find it difficult if they are overly generous to others and not to us.

Jesus is pointing out to Peter that the whole concept of "getting what you earn" is simply irrelevant when it comes to the kingdom of God. If that is what concerns us, we can rest assured that we will not get less than we have earned. The all-day workers did not get less than they earned. However, what we "get" has nothing to do with earning. It is all gift. Even the all-day workers did not earn the opportunity to go into the vineyard in the first place. They were invited. Everyone in the story is gifted beyond anything he or she earned.

We often respond to God in the same way that the laborers responded to the landowner. We grumble because we think that God is being "too generous" to others, and at the same time we fail to realize that God is also being "too generous" to us.

7. Luke 8:36–49   God forgives so we must forgive

Some people are very resistant to the idea that neither we nor our enemies get what we deserve; we get much more than we deserve. They want those who teach Scripture to emphasize God's anger and God's "just punishment" because they believe that fear of punishment is the only thing that will keep people from continuing to sin. They also like to believe that they themselves are very good and have no real need for forgiveness.

Such an attitude has negative effects both for those who hold it and for all those with whom they come in contact. We see Jesus confronting such a self-righteous, judgmental person when he is invited to be a guest at the home of Simon, a Pharisee. As Jesus and his host are reclining at table, a "sinful woman" comes in and starts to express her love for Jesus by bathing his feet with her tears. Simon thinks that if Jesus were a prophet, he would know that the woman is a sinner and would not allow her to treat him in this way. Jesus knows what Simon is thinking, so he tells Simon a parable about two debtors, one with a huge debt, the other with a small debt. Both are forgiven. Jesus asks Simon which debtor will love the master more. Simon answers, "The one, I suppose, whose larger debt was forgiven" (Lk 8:43). Jesus then compares the woman to the one whose larger debt was forgiven, and points out to Simon that the woman is more able to love than is Simon himself. Why? Because she has been forgiven. It is because she has experienced forgiveness that she is able to love. She does not earn forgiveness by loving. She becomes capable of loving because she has received forgiveness even though it is undeserved.

In comparing the woman to one debtor Jesus is, of course, comparing Simon to the other debtor. Simon feels superior and judgmental toward the woman. Simon fails to love because he has no sense of having been forgiven, or of even needing forgiveness.

God has already forgiven. The message which sinners, including ourselves, need to hear is not that we should fear God's punishment but that we should open ourselves up to accepting the forgiveness and love that God is constantly offering. Knowing that we are loved is a far more powerful incentive to turn away from sin than is fear.

8. Luke 15:11–32   We must love the sinner

The sense that other people are sinners and deserve punishment while we ourselves are good and deserve reward is, all by itself, a clear symptom of something being seriously wrong with our spiritual life. This attitude, exhibited by Simon the Pharisee, is the attitude revealed by the behavior of many of the scribes, chief priests, Pharisees and elders who appear in the Gospels. Such an attitude, then and now, makes a person unreceptive to Jesus. Jesus once told some chief priests and elders that tax collectors and prostitutes were entering the kingdom before they were (see Mt 21:31).

The reason why this attitude is so deadly to the spiritual life is not because God will punish us for it but because we will become incapable of love. Jesus tries to teach the Pharisees the danger to them of a self-righteous, judgmental attitude when he tells them the story of the man who has two sons. The younger son asks his father to give him his share of the inheritance. The father does, and the son goes off and wastes it all on a life of dissipation. After the inheritance is completely gone and the son is in need, he decides to return to his father where, even if he is treated as a servant, he will be better off. The father sees his son coming from a distance and rushes out to welcome him home. The father cannot contain his joy at his son's return, so he lavishes him with love and plans a huge celebration. The older brother, who has not done anything wrong in the first place, is angered by his father's joyful reaction. He refuses to come into their home. The father loves both sons, so he once again goes out to talk to the son who is now separating himself.

The older brother cannot hide his inability to love. He says, "...But when your son returns who swallowed up your property with prostitutes, for him you slaughter the fattened calf" (Lk 15:31). "Your son." He cannot say, "my brother." The father gently points this out when he says, "But now we must celebrate and rejoice, because your brother was dead and has come to life again; he was lost and has been found" (Lk 15:32).

Jesus tells this story to the Pharisees and scribes who are complaining because Jesus "welcomes sinners and eats with them" (Lk 15:2). The Pharisees compare to the older brother who, because he has not disobeyed any of his father's orders, has the sense that he has earned more than his brother. Like the older brother, the Pharisees are able to recognize the sins of others, but are not able to recognize their own sin. Like the older brother, the Pharisees' self-righteous and judgmental attitudes are causing them to separate themselves not only from their "brothers," but from their Father as well.

It is terribly ironic that the Pharisees complain so much about Jesus eating with sinners. Jesus did eat with sinners all the time. He ate with sinners when he ate with them. It is equally ironic when we believe that God should judge harshly and punish the sins of others, but feel that God should give us our due reward. We are wrong on both counts. God has forgiven all of us, and none of us has earned the forgiveness which we have already received.

9. Luke 23:24   Jesus forgives his executioners

Luke not only pictures Jesus teaching forgiveness, he pictures Jesus practicing forgiveness, even forgiving those who are responsible for killing him. Jesus forgives to reveal God's love. We, too, must forgive to reveal God's love. When God demands that we always love and always forgive (see Lk 17:4), God is not demanding that we be more loving and forgiving than God. God always loves and forgives. Therefore, we must do the same.

10. 2 Corinthians 5:18–22   Our ministry of reconciliation

Once we have understood the Bible's clear message of God's love, and have experienced that love and forgiveness, we have the responsibility to make this love and forgiveness known to others. The love of Christ compels us (see 2 Cor 5:14). Paul describes our ministry of reconciliation in these words: "And all this is from God, who has reconciled us to himself through Christ and given us the ministry of reconciliation, namely, God was reconciling the world to himself in Christ, not counting their trespasses against them and entrusting to us the message of reconciliation. So we are ambassadors for Christ, as if God were appealing through us. We implore you on behalf of Christ, be reconciled to God" (2 Cor 5:18–20).

It is in order to let others experience the love and forgiveness of God that Jesus taught his disciples to act as Jesus himself did. If we fail to love and forgive others, those who do not yet know Christ will be deprived of an opportunity to come to know Christ. We are Christ's ambassadors of reconciliation.

11. 1 John 4:16–19   God is love. Have no fear.

So far we have seen that the core good news of Scripture, both Old Testament and New, is that God is love. We have seen that we do not have to earn this love. It is given to us as a gift. We need only respond with faith and love. Nor do we have any reason to fear judgment. While the inevitable ramification of sin is suffering, it is God's will that we be reconciled and saved. Since we are loved, we are required to love others, even our enemies, not out of fear of punishment but just because love begets love.

All of this is summed up in a single passage in the first letter of John: "God is love, and whoever remains in love remains in God and God in him. In this is love brought to perfection among us, that we have confidence on the day of judgment because as he is, so are we in this world. There is no fear in love, but perfect love drives out fear because fear has to do with punishment, and so one who fears is not yet perfect in love. We love because he first loved us" (1 Jn 4:16–19). Because God is love we need have no fear.

So far in this book we have demonstrated that the Bible teaches us that God is love. Therefore, we need fear nothing, not even the end of the world. We have explained how to correctly interpret passages which some misunderstand and use to teach a God who is less than loving, and have focused on passages which clearly teach of God's love. In our next chapter we will address the questions: Where is Christ now? Is this time after the resurrection, and before the second coming, a time when Christ is absent? When we think of Christ's second coming, should we be completely focused on the future, or should we look also at the present? What exactly does Scripture tell us about this in-between time in which we are living?

Chapter 5

Has Christ Delayed
His Second Coming?

T here is no question that Jesus' earliest followers expected his second coming during their own lifetime. We see evidence of this in both the synoptic Gospels and in the letters.

Evidence in the Synoptic Gospels

In the Gospels of Mark, Matthew, and Luke, Jesus is pictured as giving an apocalyptic sermon (see Mk 13:1–32; Mt 24:1–36; Lk 21:5–33). The sermons are called "apocalyptic" because they use apocalyptic imagery to describe an "end time." All three accounts begin with Jesus and his disciples speaking about the temple. Jesus warns his disciples that the day will come when not a single stone of the temple will be left standing. Everything will be destroyed. In Matthew's account, the disciples then ask Jesus, "Tell us, when is this going to happen, and what will be the sign of your coming and of the end of the world?" (Mt 24:3).

Jesus then goes on to speak about the destruction of Jerusalem and about the coming of the "Son of Man." As we mentioned in Chapter 3, the image of the "Son of Man" coming on the clouds of heaven to judge the nations is borrowed from the apocalyptic book of Daniel (see Dn 12:4). Jesus says, "Immediately after the tribulation of those days, the sun will be darkened, and the moon will not give its light, and the stars will fall from the sky, and the powers of the heavens will be shaken. And then the sign of the Son of Man will appear in heaven, and all the tribes of the earth will mourn, and they will see the Son of Man coming upon the clouds of heaven with power and great glory. And he will send out his angels with a trumpet blast, and they will gather his elect from the four winds, from one end of the heavens to the other....Amen, I say to you, this generation will not pass away until all these things have taken place. Heaven and earth will pass away, but my words will not pass away" (Mt 24:29–31, 34).

All of this cosmic imagery is familiar to anyone who has read apocalyptic literature. We saw exactly the same kind of descriptions in the book of Revelation. The claim that the sun, moon, stars, the whole earth, and even the heavens will be shaken by what happens is typical apocalyptic imagery. In describing the horrible nature of a particular persecution in a specific locality, the author of apocalyptic literature uses cosmic imagery in order to make clear the totally disastrous nature of the situation for those who are caught up in it. Their whole world is destroyed. Was Jesus, then, referring merely to the destruction of the temple and of Jerusalem, which did take place in 70 A.D? All three of the synoptic Gospels reached the form in which we now have them after the destruction of Jerusalem, yet these passages were still included. A spectacular coming of the "Son of Man" was expected, and soon.

Evidence in Paul's Letters

Paul, too, expected a spectacular second coming to be imminent. Paul obviously preached such a second coming during his second missionary journey while in Thessalonica. Evidence for this statement lies in his first letter to the Thessalonians, which Paul wrote from Corinth in 51 A.D. The Thessalonians were anxiously awaiting the coming of the Lord. However, some of the newly converted Christians had died before the expected coming. This left a question in the minds of those who were still alive: Did their fellow converts miss out on the second coming? Or, when Christ comes, will he gather up the dead as well as the living? Paul assures the Thessalonians that they have nothing to fear. "We do not want you to be unaware, brothers, about those who have fallen asleep, so that you may not grieve like the rest, who have no hope. For if we believe that Jesus died and rose, so too will God, through Jesus, bring with him those who have fallen asleep. Indeed, we tell you this, on the word of the Lord, that we who are alive, who are left until the coming of the Lord, will surely not precede those who have fallen asleep. For the Lord himself, with a word of command, with the voice of an archangel and with the trumpet of God, will come down from heaven, and the dead in Christ will rise first. Then we who are alive, who are left, will be caught up together with them in the clouds to meet the Lord in the air. Thus we shall always be with the Lord. Therefore, console one another with these words" (1 Thes 4:13–18).

Paul again expresses his belief that the second coming will be spectacular and soon in his first letter to the Corinthians. "Behold, I tell you a mystery. We shall not all fall asleep, but we will all be changed, in an instant, in the blink of an eye, at the last trumpet. For the trumpet will sound, the dead will be raised incorruptible, and we shall be changed" (1 Cor 15:51–52).

"Well, where is this coming?"

As the first century drew to a close, and the spectacular second coming of the "Son of Man" did not occur, people began to ask, "Well, where is this coming?" Scripture itself responds to the question. Since many today are asking the same question, we should listen carefully to what Scripture has to say.

2 Peter

One canonical book which addresses the question is 2 Peter. Scripture scholars believe that 2 Peter is the last of the New Testament letters to be written. The end of the century author who wrote 2 Peter uses a well-known literary form of the day, a "last will and testament," to respond to some "scoffers" who are questioning Christian teachings. The author imagines Peter, who had died many years earlier and is recognized by all as a foundational figure in the Church, to be approaching the end of his life and using the occasion to teach what he knows the Church needs to hear. To attribute his teaching to Peter is not dishonest. The author is not trying to mislead anyone. He is employing a

---

REASONS FOR DATING 2 PETER LATE

- The author incorporates Jude—a later letter itself.

- The author refers to Paul's letters as a collected group. Paul's letters were collected late in the century.

LITERARY CONVENTIONS USED IN 2 PETER

- *Pseudonymity:* The author attributes his work to a venerable figure of the past and adopts that persona as the narrative voice.

- *A Last Will and Testament:* The author selects as the fictive occasion for his letter the imminent death of that purported author. That person thus writes his "last will and testament," his definitive teaching.

---

convention of the time to claim that his teaching is rooted in the teaching of the eminent apostle. The letter is obviously written after Peter's death since it refers to Paul's letters as a collection (2 Pet 3:15–16). Paul's letters were not collected until late in the century. The author of 2 Peter is responding to the needs of the Church at the end of the first century. The fact that the letter is included in the canon shows that what the author had to say is pertinent, then and now.

Among the questions which the scoffers are asking is, "Where is the promise of his coming? From the time when our ancestors fell asleep, everything has remained as it was from the beginning of creation" (2 Pet 3:4). The author of 2 Peter tells these scoffers that the reason that the second coming has not occurred is not that the expectation of a second coming is wrong. Rather, it is that God is delaying so that everyone can be saved. "The Lord does not delay his promise, as some regard 'delay,' but he is patient with you, not wishing that any should perish but that all should come to repentance" (2 Pet 3:9). The day of the Lord will come, however, so the scoffers should repent and be ready.

The Gospel of John

A second book which responds to the disillusionment caused by the fact that the expected spectacular coming of the Son of Man just hadn't happened is the Gospel of John. Like 2 Peter, John's Gospel dates to late in the first century. John's audience was asking, "Where is the Lord?" They had expected the second coming long before their time. One can understand how John's audience envied those who had known the historical Jesus, and those who would be present for the second coming, for they were the generations that had the privilege of actually experiencing the presence of Christ.

John responds to the question differently than does 2 Peter. John wants his audience to understand that the risen Christ is just as present to them as the historical Jesus was to his contemporaries and as the "Son of Man on the clouds of heaven" will be to a future generation. The whole point of the resurrection is that Jesus is presently alive and with his people. John writes his Gospel to help his audience see that Christ is present now. For this reason, John's Gospel does not picture a second coming at the end of the world at all. The "second coming" which John tries to help us see is the presence of Jesus in the Church and in the sacraments.

John's Allegorical Method

In Chapter 2 we discussed the difference between a parable and an allegory. At that time we said that an allegory has two levels of meaning, a literal level and an intentional level. The plot elements on the literal level all stand for something on the intentional level. If you read an allegory and do not realize that you are reading an allegory, you completely miss the intent of the author because you never understand the intentional level.

John's Gospel employs allegory. While it appears to be a narrative about the historical Jesus, it is actually about the risen Christ. John gives his readers many clues so that we will realize that we are supposed to look for a deeper level of meaning in his words. For one thing, John lets the divinity of Jesus shine through in all the descriptions of Jesus during his public ministry. In John's Gospel, Jesus is all-knowing, and he is always in charge. Jesus is never portrayed as a victim who feels deserted by his followers and even by God, or who prays to be relieved of his suffering. Rather, Jesus eagerly embraces his suffering. In John, Jesus' death is his victory, because through it he has accomplished what he has been sent to do.

A second way in which John urges us to think allegorically is that he introduces a number of characters who misunderstand Jesus. These characters take Jesus' words literally when Jesus intends to speak metaphorically. For instance, Jesus tells Nicodemus that a person must be born of water and the spirit in order to enter the kingdom of heaven. Nicodemus takes Jesus' words literally and asks how a man can be born again. Can he climb back in his mother's womb? Jesus, of course, is not talking about physical birth but about spiritual birth—baptism (see Jn 3:1–13).

In another conversation, Jesus tells the woman at the well that he would give her living water. She asks how this would be possible since Jesus does not even have a bucket. Again, Jesus had not intended his words to be taken literally. The woman's misunderstanding gives Jesus the opportunity to explain that the water he will give "will become a spring welling up into eternal life" (Jn 4:14), again a reference to baptism.

When we read these scenes, John intends us to understand that he is not writing just about the historical Jesus and Nicodemus, or the historical Jesus and the woman at the well. Rather, he is writing about the risen Jesus and what the risen Christ would do for those who are alive at the end of the first century. The risen Christ would give them living water. We will illustrate this double level of meaning in John's account soon when we take a close look at several passages in John's Gospel.

Still a third way in which John clues us in to the fact that we must look for an allegorical level of meaning to his narrative is that he alters some plot elements from the synoptic tradition in order to interpret the significance of what Jesus has accomplished in the life of John's readers. From the very beginning, John pictures John the Baptist recognizing Jesus as "the Lamb of God who takes away the sin of the world" (see Jn 1:29, 36). In order to follow through on the image of Jesus as the lamb of God, John moves the events of Holy Week up twenty-four hours. That is, instead of picturing Jesus' last supper with his apostles as being the Passover meal, John pictures the last meal being twenty-four hours earlier. Therefore, when Jesus is killed the day after that meal, Jesus is being slaughtered at the same time at which the lambs are being slaughtered for the Passover meal (see Jn 19:42). Obviously John is not inviting us to launch into a discussion about which version is historically accurate. If we do that, we miss his point entirely. Rather, John wants us to interpret his account allegorically in order to perceive his deeper meaning.

John's Gospel does not picture all of the miracles and exorcisms which appear in the synoptic Gospels. Rather, John tells us about only seven mighty signs which Jesus performs. Five of the seven, all but the wedding feast at Cana and the raising of Lazarus, recall stories from the synoptics. Nevertheless, when reading his Gospel, John invites us to look beyond the literal level of his account. What John intends to teach his audience lies at the allegorical level.

There is practically no passage in John which we could not use to illustrate John's method and message. However, we will limit ourselves to four: the cure of the nobleman's son, the multiplication of the loaves, Jesus' walking on water, and the cure of the man born blind.

The Cure of the Nobleman's Son

The cure of the nobleman's son is the second of Jesus' seven mighty signs in John's Gospel. As the story begins, the author reminds us of the first sign. "Then he returned to Cana in Galilee, where he had made the water wine" (Jn 4:46). If you are thinking allegorically, as John would have you think, a wedding would remind you of the relationship between God and God's people. Water and wine would remind you of baptism and eucharist. The conversation with Nicodemus about being born again of water and the Spirit would confirm in your mind that as John told the story of the wedding at Cana, he was, at the allegorical level, teaching his audience that Jesus has initiated a new spiritual order, one which is available to John's audience through baptism and eucharist. John's audience (and we) are the guests at the wedding for

THE EFFECT OF JOHN'S ALLEGORICAL METHOD

I. The material word becomes a sign of Christ's presence.

water
bread
light
wine
health (absence of sickness)
life
food

} All
symbolize
Christ's
presence

"All that came to be had life in him" (Jn 1:1).

II. Everyday experiences become signs of Christ's presence.

Thirst symbolizes longing for Christ.
Hunger symbolizes longing for Christ.
Love reflects the presence of Christ.
Words remind one of the Christ who reveals the Father.
Freedom reminds one of the effects of Christ's passion.
Safety reminds one of Jesus' care.
Fruitfulness reflects union with Christ.

III. Conclusion: Don't look just to history to find Christ. Look to your present experience.

"Now we no longer believe because of what you told us; we have heard him ourselves and we know that he really is the Savior of the world"(Jn 4:42).

whom Jesus has provided abundantly, saving the "best wine," the sacraments, until last.

During Jesus' return to Cana, a royal official, whose son is ill, approaches Jesus and asks him to "come." That is, of course, what John's audience is asking of the risen Christ. Jesus responds, "Unless you people see signs and wonders, you will not believe" (Jn 4:48). At the literal level, this response seems almost cruel. The poor man is asking for a healing for his son. Why does Jesus respond by reprimanding not only him but "you people"? If we think allegorically, however, the meaning is clear. Jesus stands for the risen Christ. The royal official stands for those in John's audience who want Jesus to come, who experience the lack of the second coming as a lack of Christ's power and presence in their lives. The risen Christ is asking John's audience why they need signs and wonders in order to believe. Instead of doing as the man asks, Jesus says, "You may go; your son will live" (Jn 4:50). The man believes what Jesus says and leaves. On his way home he learns that his son indeed does live.

Through this second mighty sign John is teaching his audience that once they have been born again through baptism (the teaching of the first sign at Cana), they must walk in faith, as did the nobleman. The fact that the risen Christ does not "come" in the way that they expect does not mean that they cannot experience Christ's power and presence. The risen Christ is powerful and present in their lives even though he is not physically present.

The Multiplication of the Loaves

The story of the multiplication of the loaves appears in all four gospels (see Mk 6:31–44; 8:1–10; Mt 14:13–21; 15:32–39; Lk 9:10–17; Jn 6:1–16). While the core of the story remains the same, the details of the story differ from one Gospel to another. As we have already learned, we must resist the temptation to ignore such differences or to explain them away. Instead, we should notice the differences and ask, "Why did this Gospel editor choose to tell the story this way?" Only when we respond to this question will we learn what the Gospel editor is trying to teach us.

In John, we notice that the feast of Passover is near. The mighty signs which Jesus performs in John's Gospel consistently take place against the backdrop of a Jewish feast. This is John's way of saying that the old spiritual order, which was ritualized through Jewish feasts, is being replaced by a new spiritual order.

The crowds are present because they have seen the "signs" which Jesus has done on the sick. While they have seen the signs, they have not understood the significance of the signs. (This is also true of John's audience.) They do not understand what the signs say about the identity of Jesus. Also, in John, Jesus "gives thanks" for the bread. The Greek word for "thanks" is *eucharisteo*. Finally, in John, Jesus does not give the bread to the disciples to distribute to the crowd. Rather, he distributes it himself.

As in every allegory in John, Jesus stands for the risen Christ. The disciples stand for the Church. The crowd stands for those hungry for spiritual nourishment. Jesus is pictured as giving thanks to remind us of the eucharist. Jesus himself distributes the bread because he himself is the bread of life. Through this allegory John is teaching his audience that Christ is present to them in the eucharist just as surely as the historical Jesus was present to his contemporaries. The risen Christ is still feeding John's audience (and us).

As is always true in John's Gospel, the allegorical significance of the sign is later taught in a dialogue. Those with whom Jesus is speaking are unable to understand what Jesus is saying, so Jesus has the opportunity to explain further. The allegorical significance of the multiplication of the loaves is explained in Jesus' "bread of life" dialogue/monologue (see Jn 6:22–71). The crowds pursue Jesus to Capernaum. Jesus tells the crowd, "Do not work for food that perishes but for the food that endures for eternal life, which the Son of Man will give you" (Jn 6:27). Notice this reference to the "Son of Man." This is the figure who is expected on the clouds of heaven. The crowd responds just as did the woman at the well. They want the bread, but they still have no idea what Jesus is talking about. Then Jesus says, "I am the bread of life; whoever comes to me will never hunger, and whoever believes in me will never thirst" (Jn 6:35). As the dialogue continues Jesus insists, "I am the living bread that came down from heaven; whoever eats this bread will live forever; and the bread that I will give is my flesh for the life of the world....Amen, amen, I say to you, unless you eat the flesh of the Son of Man and drink his blood, you do not have life within you. Whoever eats my flesh and drinks my blood has eternal life, and I will raise him on the last day" (Jn 6:51, 53–54).

John's audience is waiting for the Son of Man to come down from heaven and to gather his people up with him for eternal life. Here, Jesus insists that his followers must believe in him and must eat the flesh of the Son of Man in order to have eternal life. Through the dialogue John is teaching that the Son of Man has come down from heaven. The Son of Man is giving John's audience his flesh to eat in the eucharist. The Son of Man is giving them eternal life. All their hopes are being fulfilled. They would understand this if only they could see the significance of the signs.

Jesus Walks on the Water

Inserted between the account of the multiplication of the loaves and the dialogue which explains its eucharistic significance is the story of Jesus walking on the water. Jesus has withdrawn to the mountain, alone. The disciples get in a boat in order to go to Capernaum. It is dark. In John, darkness always means that one does not yet know the full significance of the events surrounding Jesus. It is dark when Nicodemus seeks out Jesus, and dark when Mary Magdalene goes to the tomb. John tells us that "Jesus had not yet come to them" (Jn 6:17). (Once again, at the allegorical level, John names the problem for his audience: Jesus has not come in the way in which they expected.) Not only is it dark, but a strong wind is blowing, making the sea rough. Life's journey is very rough if one feels separated from Christ. After the disciples have rowed some distance, they see Jesus walking on the sea. Jesus says, "It is I. Do not be afraid" (Jn 6:20). The disciples want to take Jesus into the boat with them, but the boat immediately arrives at the shore to which they are heading.

Jesus' assurance, "It is I," would have had a significance for John's audience which it may not have for us. Throughout his Gospel, John pictures Jesus making a number of "I am" or "It is I" statements, statements that would have recalled for a Jewish audience the words "I am" which God used to identify God's self to Moses at the burning bush. These words on Jesus' lips are a claim that Jesus is God.

As in each of John's allegories, Jesus stands for the risen Christ,

---

SOME "I AM," "IT IS I," AND "I AM..."
PASSAGES IN JOHN'S GOSPEL

4:26	"I am he."
6:20	"It is I. Do not be afraid."
6:35	"I am the bread of life."
8:12	"I am the light of the world."
8:24	"I am he."
8:28	"I am he."
8:58	"I AM."
10:7	"I am the gate of the sheepfold."
10:11	"I am the good shepherd."
10:36	"I am the Son of God."
11:25	"I am the resurrection."
13:13	"So I am."
13:19	"I am he."
14:6	"I am the way, the truth and the life."
15:1	"I am the true vine."
18:6	"I am he."
18:8	"I am he."
18:37	"I am a king."

---

who is God. The disciples stand for John's audience, who feel separated from Jesus and think that they cannot be reunited to him until they reach shore. The boat trip across rough seas symbolizes life's journey when one feels separated from Christ. The fact that the disciples would have taken Jesus into the boat, but couldn't because they had suddenly reached their destination, stands for the fact that once Jesus' disciples recognize the presence of the risen Christ in their lives, the rough journey in the dark is over. Through his allegory John is teaching his audience that they are not really separated from the risen Christ at all. They are not alone on life's journey.

The allegorical significance of this sign is reaffirmed in the dialogue/monologue which Jesus has with his apostles at the last supper. Jesus says, "I will not leave you desolate. I will come to you. Yet a little while and the world will see me no more, but you will see me; because I live, you will live also" (Jn 14:18–19). In John, as we will soon discuss, Jesus' promise to return is fulfilled in his post-resurrection appearances. John is trying to help his audience see that the risen Christ has returned and is in their midst.

Jesus Gives Sight to the Man Born Blind

John continues to try to open the eyes of his end-of-the-century audience as he tells the story of Jesus giving sight to a man born blind. At the literal level, Jesus encounters a man who has been blind since birth. The man does not ask to be healed, nor does he initially express any faith in Jesus. However, Jesus puts a mud paste on his eyes and tells him to wash in the pool of Siloam. The man does as he is instructed and is then able to see. From this point on, the story is about who can see and who cannot see. However, the drama is not about physical sight; it is about spiritual sight. It is about who can see the risen Christ. By the end of the drama, the man born blind can see in a completely different way than he could when he first regained his physical sight. At the allegorical level, the man stands for those in John's audience who come to see Christ. The Pharisees, who think they can see, and claim to be able to see, turn out to be blind. The Pharisees stand for those who refuse to see the risen Christ.

The behavior of the man born blind illustrates the gradual coming to understanding and faith of a true disciple of Jesus. An event occurs in the man's life which is completely beyond his own understanding. Although he was born blind, he can now see. In reaction to this event, the man's neighbors, the Pharisees, the Jews, and his parents are all drawn into a discussion about the identity of Jesus. Initially, when the man born blind is asked who opened his eyes, he can say only that it was "the man called Jesus." That is all he knows. However, as the Pharisees press him, the man goes a little farther. He declares that Jesus is a prophet.

Dissatisfied with his answers, the Jews decide to question the parents about how their son is now able to see. The parents say that they do not know who opened their son's eyes. The narrator's voice then tells us, "His parents said this because they were afraid of the Jews, for the Jews had already agreed that if anyone acknowledged him as the messiah, he would be expelled from the synagogue" (Jn 9:22). This

ALLEGORICAL SIGNIFICANCE OF THE SEVEN SIGNS IN JOHN'S GOSPEL

Sign—material world	Significance—spiritual world
1. Water changed to wine at Cana	At baptism we become a new creation.
2. Cure of nobleman's son	We must have faith to grow in Christ.
3. Cure of man at pool in Bethesda	The risen Christ, through his Church, still has power to forgive sins.
4. Miracle of the loaves	The eucharist, Jesus' body and blood, gives spiritual nourishment.
5. Jesus walks on water	The risen Christ is always with us.
6. Cure of the man born blind	Christ is our light—he reveals the truth and shows us the way to the Father.
7. Raising of Lazarus	Our rebirth in baptism and life in Christ lead to eternal life.

INTERWEAVING OF ALLEGORICAL SIGNS AND SOME RELATED DIALOGUES IN JOHN'S GOSPEL

2:1–12	First Sign—Wedding at Cana
3:1–21	Dialogue with Nicodemus about being "born" again
4:5–26	Dialogue with woman at the well about living "water"
4:27–38	Dialogue with disciples about Jesus' "food"
4:43–54	Second Sign—Cure of Nobleman's Son
5:1–9	Third Sign—Cure of Man at Pool of Bethesda
5:19–47	Dialogue with Jews about Jesus as judge
6:1–15	Fourth Sign—Miracle of the Loaves
6:16–21	Fifth Sign—Jesus Walks on Water
6:26–40	Dialogue with crowd about Jesus as the "bread" of life
6:41–66	Dialogue with Jews about Jesus as the "bread" of life
7:12	Dialogue with people about Jesus as the "light" of the world
9:1–7	Sixth Sign—Cure of the Man Born Blind
9:4–5, 13–41	Dialogue about Jesus as "light" and spiritual "blindness"
11:1–44	Seventh Sign—Raising of Lazarus
11:21–27	Dialogue with Martha about eternal life

Preceded by a Liturgical Hymn (1:1–18)

Followed by an account of the preparation for the passion (12:1–17:26), the passion itself (18:1–19:42), and the resurrection (20:1–21:25) statement is one of John's invitations to interpret this story at the allegorical level. If the "time context" of the story were understood to be the time of the historical Jesus, this statement would not make sense. No one was being expelled from the synagogue for claiming that Jesus was the messiah during Jesus' historic ministry.

However, if the "time context" is understood to be the time of John's audience, this statement makes perfect sense. By the time John is writing, those Jews who believed in the divinity of Jesus were being expelled from the synagogue by those Jews who did not believe in the divinity of Christ. To be expelled from the synagogue was a terrible thing because it put one's life in danger. As long as Jews were involved in the synagogue, they were excused from emperor worship. Once expelled, however, they were no longer excused and so became subject to persecution if they refused to honor the emperor as though he were God.

At the allegorical level, then, John is talking about the risen Christ's presence in the life of those living at the end of the century. He is talking about the fact that they, too, have been washed (baptized), and can now "see," and that their "sight" should enable them to arrive at the same conclusion to which the blind man will come.

Having received no satisfaction from the parents, the Jews come to the man born blind a second time. This time, in the face of their questions and accusations, the man born blind is able to state with conviction that Jesus has to be from God. "It is unheard of that anyone ever opened the eyes of a person born blind. If this man were not from God, he would not be able to do anything" (Jn 9:32–33).

Finally, Jesus seeks out the man and asks him, " 'Do you believe in the Son of Man?' He answered and said, 'Who is he, sir, that I may believe in him?' Jesus said to him 'You have seen him and the one speaking with you is he.' He said, 'I believe, Lord,' and he worshiped him" (Jn 9:35–38).

What the historical Jesus is pictured as saying to the man born blind is what John wants his audience to realize the risen Christ is saying to them. John's audience is waiting for the second coming, the coming of the "Son of Man." Remember, this is an apocalyptic image. The Son of Man is the figure pictured as coming on the clouds of heaven. But Jesus tells the man who can now see (i.e. the risen Christ is telling John's audience), "You have seen him and the one speaking with you is he."

As he recounts this story, then, John is challenging his Jewish contemporaries who are Christians to "see," to understand that Jesus is divine, and that the risen Christ is presently in their midst. They must not compromise their beliefs to avoid expulsion from the synagogue. Like the man who now sees, they must worship Jesus. Jesus is just as present to them through the Church and through what we have come to call the sacraments (i.e. baptism) as the historical Jesus was present to his contemporaries. One need not wait until the second coming to be in the presence of the risen Christ.

Just as the man who can now see represents Christians called to full faith in the risen Christ, so the Pharisees represent those who claim to be able to see, but who, in fact, refuse to see.

As the story begins, the Pharisees and Jews are pictured as completely self-confident that they already understand all truth. After all, they have their law. The Pharisees believe that if a man is born blind he or his parents must be sinners. They believe that all suffering is due to sin. They also believe that if a person works on the sabbath, he too must be a sinner. Obedience to the law is the way one earns being in right relationship to God. The Pharisees hold on to their rigid beliefs even in the face of events which call their beliefs into question. They are incapable of reexamining their beliefs in light of the revelation which has been offered to them through Jesus Christ.

A man known to the Jews to have been born blind can now see. How do the Pharisees respond? Their first response is to deny that the event ever occurred. They decide that this man who can now see looks like the man who had been blind, but he is not the same person. However, the man insists that he is the same person.

The Pharisees' next response is to decide that whoever opened the man's eyes cannot be from God because he performed this mighty sign on the sabbath. If something Jesus does challenges the Pharisees' traditional beliefs, they immediately reject Jesus rather than reexamine the beliefs. However, the man born blind challenges the Pharisees on their dismissal of Jesus. How could a person perform such a mighty sign if God were not with him? Surely, Jesus is from God.

Once challenged both by the event which they themselves witnessed, and by the reasoned arguments of the man who gives personal witness to Jesus' power, the Pharisees again fall back on their traditional beliefs. They say to the man, "You were born totally in sin, and are you trying to teach us?" (Jn 9:34). The reason they accuse the man of having been born in sin is that they believe that all suffering is due to sin. So a person born blind must be a sinner or he would not have been blind in the first place. After dismissing the man as a sinner, the Pharisees throw him out.

Later, when Jesus seeks out the man born blind and reveals his identity to him, some Pharisees are also present. They witness the man worshiping Jesus. Jesus says, "I came into this world for judgment, so that those who do not see might see, and those who do see might become blind" (Jn 9:39). The Pharisees suspect that this comment about "becoming blind" might be aimed at them. They ask Jesus if he is calling them blind. Jesus replies, "If you were blind, you would have no sin; but now you are saying, 'We see,' so your sin remains" (Jn 9:41).

Obviously Jesus is referring to spiritual blindness, not physical blindness. The Pharisees choose to be spiritually blind. They refuse to acknowledge the reality of the events which they themselves have witnessed. They try to dismiss as "sinners" both those who give witness to Jesus' power in their lives and Jesus himself, denying that he is from God. These are the very qualities which John is condemning in those Jews who lived at the end of the first century, those who clung to beliefs which were held before Jesus' powerful ministry, and before Jesus' resurrection from the dead. Rather than coming to terms with these events, or believing the witness of their fellow Jews who have personally experienced Jesus' presence and power, they are denying these events, and are throwing their fellow Jews out of the synagogue. The Pharisees claim to be spiritual leaders. They claim to "see," but actually they are blind.

The question which John is posing throughout his Gospel is whether those in his audience, including us, are also blind. If we look so much to a future coming of Jesus that we do not recognize that Jesus is already in our midst, then we, too, are blind, even if we claim to see.

Post-Resurrection Appearance Stories

Earlier in this chapter we mentioned that in John's Gospel Jesus' promise to return is fulfilled in his post-resurrection appearances. At his last meal with the apostles Jesus promised that he would return. He also promised the apostles that they would share his joy. "So you also are now in anguish. But I will see you again, and your hearts will rejoice, and no one will take your joy away from you" (Jn 16:22). This promise and prayer are fulfilled when Jesus appears to the apostles after his resurrection. "On the evening of that first day of the week, when the doors were locked, where the disciples were, for fear of the Jews, Jesus came and stood in their midst and said to them 'Peace be with you.' When he had said this, he showed them his hands and his side. The disciples rejoiced when they saw the Lord" (Jn 20:19–20).

Thomas was not present when the Lord appeared, and he refused to believe the witness of his fellow apostles. Thomas acts just as John's audience is acting. He says, "Unless I see the mark of the nails in his hands and put my finger into the nailmarks and put my hand into his side, I will not believe" (Jn 20:25). Thomas wants to see and to touch the body of Christ as a physical object. Later, Jesus says to Thomas, "Have you come to believe because you have seen me? Blessed are those who have not seen and have believed" (Jn 20:29). These are the words which John wants his audience to hear the risen Christ saying to them. One need not touch the physical body of Christ to come to faith in his presence.

John has already stressed that it is love, not physical proof, which enables one to arrive at a belief in the risen Christ by his account of Peter and the beloved disciple's reactions after Mary Magdalene tells them that "they have taken the Lord from the tomb, and we don't know where they put him" (Jn 20:3). Both Peter and the beloved disciple rush to the tomb, but the beloved disciple gets there first. Both observe the wrappings, but only the beloved disciple "saw and believed." By introducing the character of the beloved disciple, a character who appears in no other Gospel, and by contrasting him to Peter, who represents both rank and authority to John's audience, John is emphasizing that the beloved disciple believed before any appearances: he believed just on the basis of love. John's audience, too, is called to believe without an appearance (i.e. the long overdue parousia.).

Soon after the empty tomb is discovered Jesus starts to appear to his followers. However, even those who knew Jesus best have difficulty recognizing him. In fact, an inability to recognize the presence of the risen Christ is a recurring theme in post-resurrection appearance stories. Remember, Mary Magdalene didn't recognize Jesus. She mistook him for a gardener (see Jn 20:11–18). Remember the disciples by the Sea of Tiberias? Jesus called out to them from the shore, but they did not know who he was (see Jn 21:1–14). Remember the two disciples on the road to Emmaus (see Lk 24:13–35)? They had a long conversation with Jesus and had no idea that it was Jesus with whom they were speaking. Obviously, this "lack of recognition" is an important part of post-resurrection appearance stories. The question is: What does it mean? What are the story tellers trying to teach us?

"I Don't Think You Recognized Me."

I had an experience two years ago that has, I believe, helped me to understand what the post-resurrection appearance stories are trying to teach us. My father had suffered a series of strokes. His last stroke had left him unable to speak or to swallow. I knew that he did not want his suffering prolonged unnecessarily. However, I signed permission for a doctor to give him a feeding tube, simply not knowing whether this was what he would have chosen had he been able to express his own desires. All that day I was thinking about the ramifications of my action. If my father were able to leave the hospital, could he go back to the apartment where he and my mother lived? Could the women who had been caring for them, who were not nurses, learn how to care for my father under these conditions?

Worrying about all of these details, I got on the elevator at the hospital. I did not look at anyone—I simply turned around with my face to the door. A voice behind me said, "I don't think you recognized me." I turned to look at a woman who did not look at all familiar to me. "I'm sorry," I said, "but I don't recognize you."

"That's no wonder," she said. "You meet lots of people and you can't remember them all. I was a sponsor in the RCIA. You spoke to us several times on Scripture. I loved your work,"

"Thank you," I replied. "What is your work?"

"I represent 'Option Home Care,' " she said. "Have you heard of us?"

"No, I haven't," I replied.

"Well, we teach people how to take care of family members at home instead of putting them in a nursing home. For instance—say someone in your family had a stroke and needed a feeding tube. We teach the family how to take care of that person."

I was dumbfounded. Immediately my story poured out. She told me not to worry. If my father came home again, she personally would see that his care givers knew what to do. She was true to her word and all went smoothly when my father came home.

A month later my father was back in the hospital with pneumonia. As time passed, I noticed that his mouth was getting crusty and his lips looked scabbed and split. I expressed my concern to the nurse on duty who snapped at me and seemed to take my comment as a personal insult. Once again I was very upset as I got on the hospital elevator. Again I turned and faced the door. The elevator door closed and the whole elevator shook. I was afraid that we were stuck between floors. However, when the doors opened again we were still on the same floor. I decided to take the stairs.

As I walked down the stairs, a voice from behind me said, "I don't think you recognized me." I turned to look and once again I did not recognize the person speaking to me. "I'm sorry, but I don't recognize you," I said.

"I took a Scripture course from you years ago," the woman said. "I love Scripture. I loved that course,"

"Thank you," I said. "And what do you do?"

"I supervise the nursing of geriatric stroke patients," she said. Once again I was astounded. Once again my story poured out. "I will go and see your father right now," she said, "and I will take care of this."

Later when I went to my father's room, his mouth was already showing marked improvement. Every morning when I went to the hospital the nurse supervisor was there, right up to the day my father died.

Now when I teach the course on Scripture that the nurse supervisor loved, I teach the appearance stories differently than I had before. I start with the stories about these good women who loved scripture, who had been baptized into Christ's body, and who said to me, "I don't think you recognized me." It is not just Mary Magdalene, the apostles on the shore, or the disciples on the road to Emmaus who fail to recognize the risen Christ. We all do. Perhaps the stories were told as they were to teach this very point.

The post-resurrection appearance stories, like John's Gospel, have a greater depth of meaning than one might understand on first reading.

These stories are probing a mystery. They are trying to tell us about the experience of the early Church. Jesus had a powerful public ministry. Jesus was killed and buried. After all of this, when Jesus should have been dead, Jesus was still alive. Jesus' disciples knew he was still alive, not because they witnessed the resurrection, but because they experienced the presence of the risen Christ. How did they experience him? The post-resurrection appearance stories probe this mystery.

The Disciples on the Road to Emmaus

One of the appearance stories involves two disciples on the road to Emmaus (see Lk 24:13–35). The two are walking along thinking and talking about Jesus. A fellow traveler joins them. The narrator's voice tells us that this fellow traveler is Jesus, "but their eyes were prevented from recognizing him" (Lk 24:16). As the story is constructed, the whole story of Jesus is recounted: Cleopas tells the stranger about Jesus' ministry, about his rejection, persecution, and death, about the disciples' dashed hopes, and about the empty tomb and the claims of resurrection.

The stranger, still not recognized, admonishes the disciples, saying, "Oh, how foolish you are! How slow of heart to believe all that the prophets spoke! Was it not necessary that the messiah should suffer these things and enter into his glory?" (Lk 24:25–26). The unrecognizable Jesus then reinterprets passages of Scripture that, in hindsight, can be understood to unlock some of the mystery surrounding Jesus, the mystery of the cross.

The narrator does not tell us which passages were reinterpreted. However, as we discussed in Chapter 3, Isaiah's passages of the suffering servant were used by the early Church in just this way. In the light of events, an additional level of meaning was discerned in the words of the prophets. By using the words, images, and concepts already present in the religious tradition, meaning was found in the most mysterious of events, the cross. Here, this practice of using images and concepts from the prophets to explain Christ's passion and death is attributed to the risen Christ himself.

Still, the fellow traveler goes unrecognized. As they approach the village, their companion "gives the impression" that he will leave them, but they urge him to stay. "So he went in to stay with them. And it happened that, while he was with them at table, he took bread, said the blessing, broke it, and gave it to them. With that their eyes were opened and they recognized him, but he vanished from their sight. Then they said to each other, 'Were not our hearts burning within us while he spoke to us on the way and opened the scriptures to us?' " (Lk 24:29–32).

.What are we to make of this strange account? What is the early Church trying to teach about the risen Christ by telling the story in this way? Are we not being taught that the risen Christ is in the fellow traveler, in the living word, and in the eucharist?

Two disciples of Christ are on the road, thinking and talking about Christ. We, too, are disciples of Christ, on the road, thinking and talking about Christ. A fellow traveler approaches. This is the story of our life. Fellow travelers are always approaching. The risen Christ is present in the fellow traveler, yet "our eyes are prevented" from recognizing Christ.

The traveler turns to Scripture to explore the mystery of Jesus Christ. We, too, turn to the Scripture, the living word, to explore the mystery of the risen Christ. Are not our hearts burning within us when we read it and begin to understand the depth of its meaning and the beauty of its message?

The traveler joins them at the table, where the bread is blessed and broken. It is here, in the breaking of the bread, that they finally recognize Christ. We, too, approach the table, where we bless and break the bread. We, too, recognize the presence of the risen Christ in the breaking of the bread.

The post-resurrection stories, like John's Gospel, are teaching us that the risen Christ is truly present in our midst, although we often fail to recognize him. Where might we find Jesus? Jesus is present in the fellow traveler, in the gardener, in the stranger calling from the shore, "Are you catching any fish?" Jesus is present in his body, the Church. Jesus is also present in the living word, in Scripture, and in the sacraments, including baptism and eucharist. We do not need to look to the future to see Jesus coming on the clouds of heaven. Jesus is with us now.

"Exactly What Happened?"

"Are you saying that Jesus did not actually appear to Mary Magdalene or to the disciples on the road to Emmaus?" This is the question which I know, from years of teaching, is on the minds of many readers.

"No, I am not saying that," is my answer. To explain this answer I will have to remind you of what we learned in Chapter 1. The revelation which the Gospels contain is based on events. Immediately after the resurrection, Jesus' disciples knew, absolutely knew through personal experience, that Jesus was still alive. The stories of Jesus' post-resurrection appearances are based on events, on personal experience.

However, the stories were not told to describe the experience. They were told to teach the significance of the experience in the lives of the believing community. The desired effect of the stories is not to pass on only a knowledge of the fact that the risen Christ appeared immediately after his resurrection to those who believed in him. The desired effect is to teach that the risen Christ is still present in the lives of those who are reading the story. So if we insist on asking the text, "Tell us exactly what happened and only what happened," we are asking the text to do something the authors did not intend it to do. The authors did not provide a record of exactly what happened and only what happened. They were using their experiences to teach of Christ's loving presence. Therefore, in order to understand the revelation which the stories contain, we must let the author of each story teach what the author intended to teach.

The Accounts of Jesus' Appearance to Paul

One way of illustrating the difference between reporting an event as it occurred and telling a story about that event in order to teach the significance of the event is to compare the three accounts of Jesus' appearance to Paul on the road to Damascus. None of these accounts tries to tell us what the experience was actually like for Paul or for those who were with Paul.

The closest we can come to knowing what Paul actually experienced is to read Paul's reference to his experience in his second letter to the

Corinthians. "I must boast; not that it is profitable, but I will go on to visions and revelations of the Lord. I know someone in Christ who, fourteen years ago (whether in the body or out of the body I do not know, God knows), was caught up to the third heaven. And I know that this person (whether in the body or out of the body I do not know, God knows) was caught up into Paradise and heard ineffable things, which no one may utter" (2 Cor 12:1–4). Here Paul is referring to the fact that the risen Christ appeared to him and that his personal experience of the risen Christ is at the base of everything he has said or done since. However, the experience he had is indescribable. He himself does not understand it. He has no words, nor do we, that would enable him to explain "exactly what happened."

However, as Paul lived out his life, and the meaning and ramifications of that experience became clear to him and to the early Church, an account of Jesus' post-resurrection appearance to Paul, and the ramifications of that event for Paul and for the Gentiles, took story form. Three variations of the story appear in the Acts of the Apostles (see Acts 9:1–19; 22:1–16; 26:9–18). The accounts have core events in common but differ in details. Through the details, the author interprets the significance of the events for the reader.

In each account, Saul (Paul) is on the road to Damascus with the intent of persecuting Jesus' followers. While he is on the road, he is surrounded by a light. Saul falls to the ground and a voice says, "Saul, Saul why do you persecute me?" Paul responds, "Who are you, Lord?" and the voice responds, "I am Jesus whom you are persecuting."

The stories differ in the way they describe what those traveling with Paul saw and heard, the role given to Ananias, and who in the story explains the significance of the event, a significance understood only in hindsight. In the first account, the explanation of the significance of the event is placed on Jesus' lips. Ananias warns the Lord against Saul, but the Lord says, "Go, for he is a chosen instrument of mine to carry my name before the Gentiles and kings and the sons of Israel..." (Acts 9:15). In the second account the explanation of Paul's vocation is placed on Ananias' lips as he speaks to Paul. In the third account Jesus once more explains Paul's vocation, but this time to Paul himself.

As we compare the stories it becomes obvious that the intent of the author is not to give us a literal description of the event as Paul experienced it, but to teach the significance of the event in the lives of the

---

THREE ACCOUNTS OF PAUL'S CONVERSION

(Acts 9:1–19; 22:1–16; 26:9–18)

Events in common

- Saul is on the road to Damascus with the intent of persecuting Jesus' followers.
- Saul is surrounded by a light.
- Saul falls to the ground.
- A voice says, "Saul, Saul, why do you persecute me?"
- Paul responds, "Who are you, Lord?"
- The voice says, "I am Jesus whom you are persecuting."

Details which differ

- What do those traveling with Paul see and hear?
- What role does Ananias play?
- What does Ananias say?
- In whose mouth does the explanation of Paul's conversion appear?

Gentile audience. Paul was God's chosen instrument to bring the good news of Christ to the Gentiles.

In the same way, the post-resurrection appearance stories are told, not to describe the events exactly as they happened, but to teach the significance of the events in the lives of those to whom the Gospels are addressed: later generations of disciples, including us.

That Our Joy May Be Complete

The experience of every generation attests to the fact that those who did not know the historical Jesus can still give witness to the bodily presence of the risen Christ. It is this mysterious truth to which the author of 1 John gives witness as he writes near the close of the first century A.D.: "We declare to you what was from the beginning, what we have heard, what we have seen with our eyes, what we have looked at and touched with our hands, concerning the word of life....This life was revealed; and we have seen it and testify to it, and declare to you the eternal life that was with the Father and was revealed to us—we declare to you what we have seen and heard so that you also may have fellowship with us; and truly our fellowship is with the Father and with his Son Jesus Christ. We are writing these things so that our joy may be complete" (1 Jn 1:1–4).

We, too, can see and touch Christ. All of the passages we have discussed in this chapter, and many more, teach us that the risen Christ is present and is establishing his kingdom as we speak. We need not look only to the future, to some cataclysmic event, to see the coming of the Lord. We can look to the here and now. Our prayer of *Marana tha* — "O Lord, come"—can become *Maran atha,* "Our Lord has come." We, like the blind man in John's Gospel, can gradually come to see. As our eyes are opened we, like Mary Magdalene, and like the apostles, will be able to say, "I have seen the Lord!"

The Lord has not delayed his coming. The Son of Man, come down from heaven, is with us now, in the Church, in the sacraments, and in each other.

END NOTE

"Are you denying the second coming?" is a question which I am often asked. My answer is, "No, I am not." A belief in a future culminating event is core to Christianity. We profess our belief in such an event when we say in the Creed that Jesus "ascended into heaven, and is seated at the right hand of the Father. He will come again in glory to judge the living and the dead."

As I write this end note it is the Easter season. Each day at Mass, as the stories of Jesus' appearances are told, the prayers interpret the stories in the context of our own lives. For instance, the opening prayer on the 7th Sunday of Easter reads, "Eternal Father, reaching from end to end of the universe, and ordering all things with your mighty arm: for you, time is the unfolding of truth that already is, the unveiling of beauty that is yet to be. Your Son has saved us in history by rising from the dead, so that transcending time he might free us from death. May his presence among us lead to the vision of unlimited truth and unfold the beauty of your love. We ask this in the name of Jesus the Lord. Amen."

"...for you, time is the unfolding of truth that already is...." Jesus is already present among us. That is why in the Eucharistic Prayer we hear, "You are truly blessed, O God of holiness: you accompany us with love as we journey through life. Blessed too is your Son, Jesus Christ, who is present among us and whose love gathers us together. As once he did for his disciples, Christ now opens the Scriptures for us and breaks the bread." The risen Christ is present with us, just as he was present with the disciples on the road to Emmaus. We have nothing to fear, not even the end of the world.

Index of Biblical References